TOURISM
ENTREPRENEURS

MELODI BOTHA

FELICITÉ FAIRER-WESSELS

BERENDIEN LUBBE

JUTA
AND COMPANY LTD

Tourism Entrepreneurs

© Juta and Co Ltd, 2006
PO Box 24309
Lansdowne 7779
Cape Town, South Africa

ISBN 07021 71697

Project management: Sarah O'Neill
Editing: Alex Potter
Proofreading: Cecily van Gend
Indexing: Cecily van Gend
Cover design: WaterBerry Designs
Designed and typeset in Frutiger 57 Condensed by WaterBerry Designs

With thanks to the following people for the use of photographs: LTU (page 11); Rovos Rail (page 13); Andrew Weir Shipping (page 15).

Printed and bound in the Republic of South Africa by Formeset Printers Cape.

CONTENTS

Preface

Entrepreneurship throughout the world is stirring a revolution that is reforming and revitalising economies because it establishes new businesses and helps to grow existing ones. Entrepreneurial activity is a prerequisite for the success of economic growth, development, social well-being, job creation and political stability in a country such as South Africa. Tourism is the world's fastest growing industry and is regarded as the one industry that can change the globe in terms of alleviating poverty through job creation. For tourism to play a pivotal role in our economy, skills must be developed at every level. Educating entrepreneurs is vital because entrepreneurs are the people who will drive our economy.

However, for this to happen you need committed, creative people who are driven to face challenges and opportunities. If the dedication and commitment is there, then anything is possible, and with this book you will be given the first steps to reach that dream. Tourism is regarded as the 'new gold' and as we become less dependent on the Earth's natural resources, we must look to people to create this 'new gold' for the benefit of all.

The authors of this book have combined tourism and entrepreneurship in a creative and comprehensive way. The authors are not only involved in teaching either entrepreneurship or tourism at a major university in South Africa, but also have solid industry-related experience in both fields. This book has been written for anyone with the passion to start his or her own business, specifically in the tourism industry. There are relevant reader-friendly text, exercises, examples and case studies that link the entrepreneur or potential entrepreneur to the tourism industry and provide guidance of how he or she can capitalise this industry.

The first part of the book focuses on defining and explaining what tourism covers, from the demand to supply, and what entrepreneurship is. It then guides the reader on where to start when looking for entrepreneurial opportunities, and how to take advantage of these. The next section offers advice on starting your own business and provides a clear indication of how to develop a business plan for your venture. The final part of the book focuses on getting together and managing the resources needed to start your business, and concludes with how to grow it through outsourcing, tendering and franchising.

We wish to thank the contributors to this book, as well as our project manager at JUTA, Sarah O'Neill.

Lastly, to the reader, we hope that you enjoy the book as much as we enjoyed bringing it to you.

Melodi Botha
Felicité Fairer-Wessels
Berendien Lubbe
September 2005

The Business of Tourism

Berendien Lubbe

Once you have worked through this chapter, you should be able to:
☞ Distinguish between tourism as an activity, as an industry and as a system
☞ Identify the components of the tourism system and how they are linked
☞ Explain the environment in which tourism operates
☞ Explain what motivates tourists to travel
☞ Explain the important role of the entrepreneur in tourism

1.1 INTRODUCTION

If someone were to ask you what you understand tourism to mean, you might give any one of a number of answers, for example:
- 'Tourism is when tourists come to South Africa to see the attractions.'
- 'Tourism is something that is good for South Africa's economic growth.'
- 'Tourism is an industry that creates jobs.'
- 'Tourism is what was worst hit in some Pacific and Asian countries by the tsunami.'
- 'Tourism is what keeps our national airline going.'
- 'Tourism is when rural people sell their wares on tourist routes.'
- 'Tourism is what travel agents do.'
- 'Tourism is an industry that is regulated by government.'
- 'Tourism is what SA Tourism does to market South Africa overseas.'

Tourism is all of these things, and many more. The World Tourism Organisation (WTO) defines tourism as follows: *Tourism comprises the activities of persons travelling to and staying in places outside their usual environment for not more than one consecutive year for leisure, business or other purposes.*

From this definition, we see that tourism is a whole host of things: it is made up of activities and experiences people have through what they do and what they feel when visiting outside of their home environment and, depending on the purpose for which they travel, can be either for holiday or business, to visit friends and family or to study.

Tourism is also made up of the businesses that form a whole **industry**; individuals, small, medium and large businesses that provide the places where tourists stay (hotels, lodges, guesthouses), the food they eat (restaurants, fast food outlets), the way in which they move from one place to another (airlines, coaches, trains), the services they buy when experiencing another place (museums, tour operators, information kiosks) and the products they buy while travelling (crafts, clothes, wine). As an industry, tourism provides jobs for both skilled and unskilled workers.

Tourism also operates in an **environment** that can affect it in different ways. On the one hand, governments impose regulations on tourists (for example, tourists require visas to visit certain countries) and on the components of the tourist industry (for example, tour coaches need certain licences to carry passengers, airlines must adhere to minimum safety regulations, businesses need operating licences, taxes must be paid). On the other hand, disasters can occur in the environment; for example, a disaster such as the tsunami of 26 December 2004 all but destroyed the tourism industry in some regions of Indonesia.

For us to understand what tourism is and where we as tourism entrepreneurs fit in, we should view tourism as a **system** with many component parts that are all interrelated and interdependent. Let us draw a model to illustrate what we mean when we say tourism is a system.

This model is depicted in Figure 1.1 and shows the four main components of the tourism system: the **environment** in which tourism operates and all the influences from various parts of the environement; why and where tourists travel (the **need** for or **demand** for tourism); the resources and industries that produce tourism products and services (tourism businesses or the **supply** of tourism); and finally, how tourist demand and tourist supply are linked, through physical means such as transportation, and functional means such as the channels used to distribute information about tourism, and allow for the purchase of the tourism product by the potential tourist (**linkages**). From this model, it is evident that tourism is an interdependent system. In other words, any destination, be it a country or an attraction within a country, is made up of demand that is created and supply that is managed; linked through transportation and distribution channels; and facilitated, regulated and affected by environmental factors.

So, to be successful as a tourism entrepreneur, you need to understand why people travel, what tourists want, what you can offer, how you can reach potential tourists and how the environment can affect your efforts to run a successful tourism business.

ENVIRONMENTAL INFLUENCES

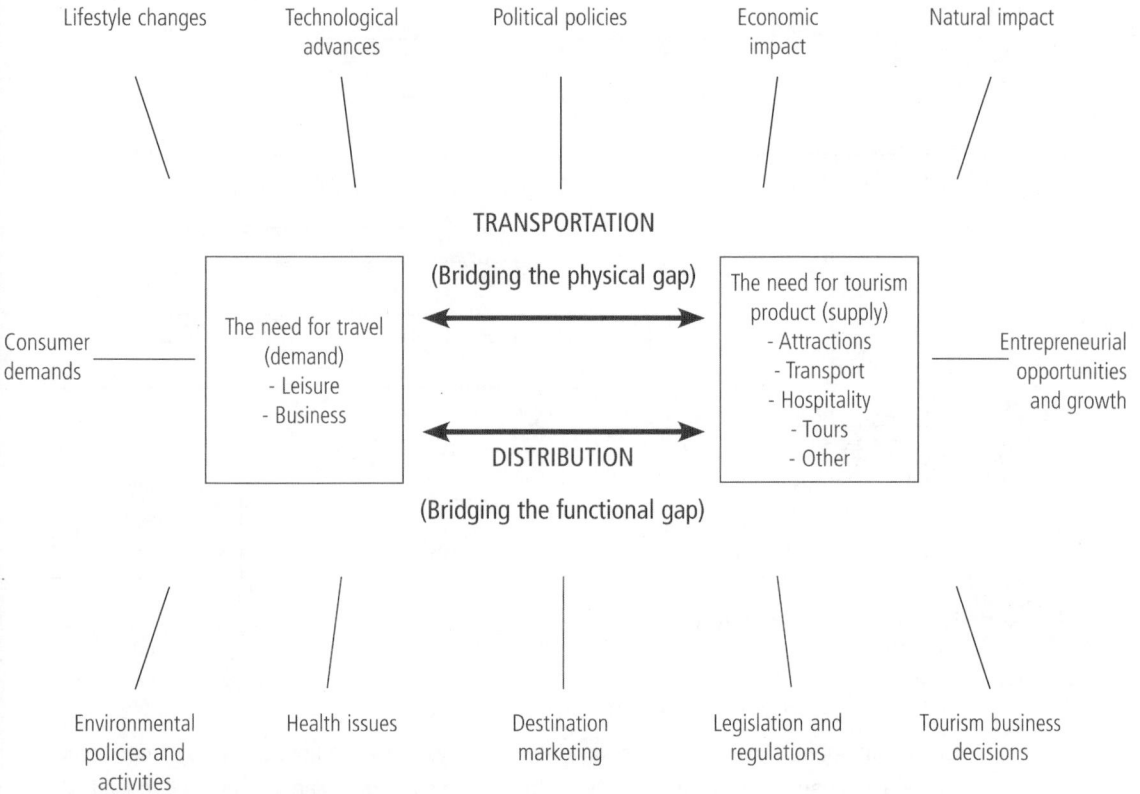

| Lifestyle changes | Technological advances | Political policies | Economic impact | Natural impact |

TRANSPORTATION

(Bridging the physical gap)

Consumer demands

The need for travel (demand)
- Leisure
- Business

←——————————→

The need for tourism product (supply)
- Attractions
- Transport
- Hospitality
- Tours
- Other

Entrepreneurial opportunities and growth

←——————————→

DISTRIBUTION

(Bridging the functional gap)

| Environmental policies and activities | Health issues | Destination marketing | Legislation and regulations | Tourism business decisions |

Figure 1.1:   **The tourism system**

Let us now look at each of the four main components of the tourism system individually: the **demand** for tourism, the **supply** of tourism, the **linkages** between supply and demand, and the **environment** within which tourism operates.

1.2   THE DEMAND FOR TOURISM

Tourism begins with the individual tourist and what he or she wants. As a tourism entrepreneur, you should realise that by understanding why tourists travel and what they need, you can fulfil those needs through a successful business. We talk about the demand for tourism when we talk about why tourists travel, where they go and what they do. Tourists that have similar interests and generally travel to the same places and do the same types of things can be grouped into so-called **market segments**. How can we practically segment tourists into groups that tourism entrepreneurs can target as potential clients? The first and probably the easiest way is to identify the purpose of travel. Tourists can be segmented according to the purpose of travel as in Figure 1.2.

```
                        ┌─────────────────────────────┐
                        │       Purpose of travel      │
                        └─────────────────────────────┘
                    ┌───────────────┴───────────────┐
          ┌─────────────────┐              ┌─────────────────┐
          │    Business      │              │     Leisure      │
          └─────────────────┘              └─────────────────┘
                                   ┌───────────┬───────────┐
                          ┌──────────────┐ ┌──────────────┐ ┌──────────────┐
                          │ Visiting      │ │ Other        │ │              │
                          │ friends or    │ │ personal     │ │   Holiday    │
                          │ relatives     │ │ business     │ │              │
                          └──────────────┘ └──────────────┘ └──────────────┘
          ┌─────────────────┐                              ┌─────────────────┐
          │ Primary          │                             │ Primary          │
          │ activities       │                             │ activities       │
          │ Meetings         │                             │ Touring          │
          │ Conferences      │                             │ Recreation       │
          │ Exhibitions      │                             │ Sightseeing      │
          └─────────────────┘                              └─────────────────┘
```

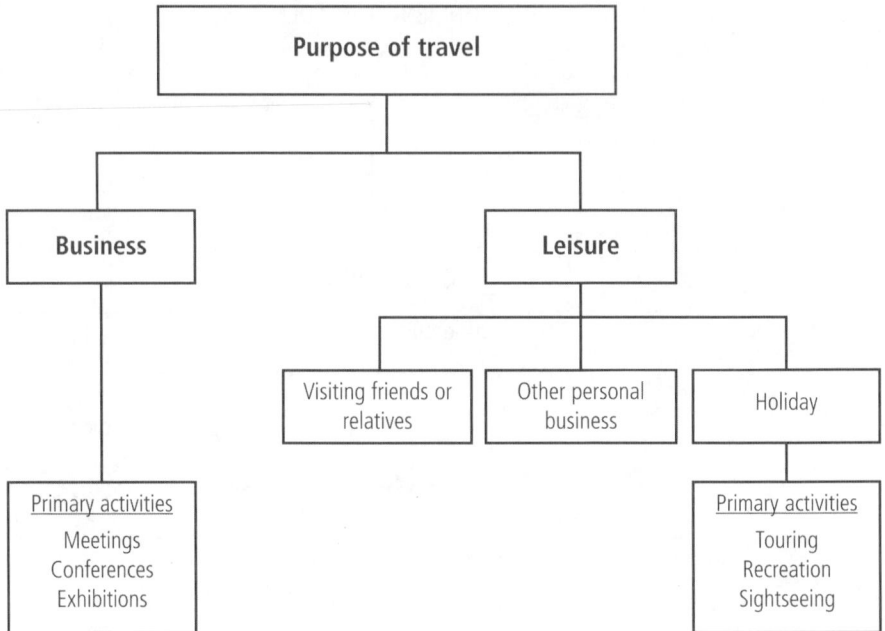

Figure 1.2:   **The purpose of travel**

1.2.1   Leisure travel in a nutshell

People can spend their leisure time in different ways either at home or away from home. Horner and Swarbrooke (2005) talk about the 'leisure consumer' and suggest that individuals fall into categories (not necessarily mutually exclusive) such as: the sportsperson (experiencing indoor or outdoor activities); the artist (learning from the arts, theatre and cinema); the hedonist (indulging in health or beauty treatments and gambling); the consumer (consuming food and drink); the spiritualist (seeking or experiencing spiritual fulfilment); the home lover (gardening; do-it-yourself); the shopper; the student (learning new facts); and the tourist (travelling away from home for more than two days). The most interesting thing about the leisure tourist is that he or she can indulge in any of these opportunities while also being a tourist. Destinations create these opportunities for tourists, and this is why some destinations become well known for their sporting activities (skiing in Austria); their shopping experience (Dubai, Hong Kong); their spiritual experience (Israel, Mecca); their gambling (Las Vegas); and their culture, arts and cinema (India, Paris, Hollywood). The leisure tourist can therefore travel away from home to experience any number of these opportunities. The most important characteristic of leisure travel is that it is discretionary; in other words, people can decide for themselves how they wish to spend the·time they have left after the time spent equipping themselves with the necessities of life (Horner & Swarbrooke, 2005:23). They can also decide for themselves how they wish to spend their discretionary income (that part of their income that is left after they have paid living expenses such as rent, food, transport and so on). As an entrepreneur, you need to understand what leisure activities tourists are interested in, how much time they have to participate in these activities and what they would be willing to pay for these opportunities and activities.

The discretionary nature of leisure travel is also what distinguishes it from business travel.

1.2.2 Business travel in a nutshell

Business travel is generally non-discretionary. People need to travel for purposes that are related to their work. This can include general business travel such as company executives travelling to sort out problems, make sales presentations and negotiate deals, or for a myriad of other reasons. People also travel on business to attend meetings, conferences, trade fairs and exhibitions, or on incentive trips. The time of travel depends on the circumstances and is not always a matter of choice. The business for which the traveller works also pays for the travel and related expenses and the individual must, in many instances, abide by the company's travel policy. Business travel and leisure travel are often combined in one trip, with a businessperson spending time on leisure activities while he/she is on a business trip. Accommodation establishments, transport facilities and even tourist attractions normally cater for both markets. A type of travel that is regarded as both business and leisure is the incentive trip, because the company pays for the trip, while the individual who has earned the trip for work achieved goes on a holiday.

1.2.3 General tourist flows

Once the decision to travel has been made, decisions on where, when and how to travel become relevant. These travel choices made by tourists are reflected in international and national travel flows. A number of organisations research the flow of tourists internationally and domestically. The WTO and the World Travel and Tourism Council (WTTC) are two international bodies that document where tourists go on a global scale and the contribution that tourism makes to a country's gross domestic product. For example, the WTTC states the following about tourism on a global scale.

In 2005, travel and tourism are expected to generate:
US$ 6 201.49 billion of economic activity
10.6% of total word GDP; and
221 568 jobs or 8.3% of total employment
(WTTC, 2005)

In South Africa, we rely on organisations such as SA Tourism and Statistics South Africa to tell us where tourists go, what places they visit, how much they spend and whether tourism is growing in South Africa.

Access the two websites given below and answer the following questions:

1. How many foreign tourists came to South Africa in 2005?
2. How many tourists were from Africa?
3. How many tourists came from the rest of the world?
4. Which countries generate the most tourists to South Africa?
5. What are the most popular places to visit in South Africa?

www.satourism.net (click on Research)
www.statssa.gov.za

These flows indicate the current demand for travel to any particular destination, which comprises attractions, transport, hospitality and infrastructure, as shown on the **supply** side of the tourism system.

1.3   THE SUPPLY OF TOURISM

A tourist destination is generally attractive to a tourist because of its unique characteristics. What would you say are the unique features of South Africa as a tourist destination? The wildlife, scenery, cultural diversity, history, wine? Yes, any one of these and many more features attract tourists. These features must be 'packaged' in such a way that they can attract visitors. Organisations, small businesses and individuals (such as tour guides) in the tourism industry try to do just that. Private and public sector businesses offer services such as transport, accommodation, cultural experiences, arts and crafts, and various tourist activities to meet the needs of tourists coming to South Africa or South Africans travelling within the country. All these businesses make up the tourism industry. The WTTC, whose primary purpose is to document the size and economic impact of travel and tourism, and which describes tourism as the world's largest industry, defines the travel and tourism industry as '*the network of businesses that are engaged in the transport, accommodation, feeding, entertainment and care of the traveller*.' In this definition, a number of elements of the tourist experience are highlighted, namely transportation, accommodation, feeding and entertainment of the tourist. Which of these is then the actual tourism product?

1.3.1   The tourism product in a nutshell

The tourism product is no single thing, but rather a bundle of all these elements and activities put together. The tourist experience can be most enjoyable if every organisation providing a part of the experience does it well, or it can be very unsatisfactory if one part of the experience is spoilt in some way. A trip can be spoilt for a tourist if he/she receives bad service on the aircraft, at the airport, at the hotel or on a touring coach; if a provider overcharges and the tourist feels he/she has been taken for a ride; if the information given to him/her by the travel agency is incorrect; or if the bank teller is rude when the tourist exchanges his/her travellers' cheques. As entrepreneurs, we must realise that we form part of a chain of activities and that, after his/her visit, the tourist can decide to recommend a trip to South Africa to others on the basis of our performance and interaction. The tourist is not buying a single product, but rather a bundle of products and services, all interlinked. At the core of this bundle of activities lies the uniqueness of the destination: that which motivated the tourist to select South Africa as a destination for his/her visit.

South Africa has a rich natural and cultural heritage and all involved in bringing tourists to South Africa and helping to make their visit to South Africa a wonderful experience must follow ecologically sound principles, so that South Africa retains its unique character as a tourist destination. This means that we must manage our natural and cultural resources in such a way that tourists are sensitive to what we have to offer and understand how important it is to keep these resources sustainable for future generations. In the tourism system depicted in Figure 1.1, the 'supply' side of tourism includes the natural and cultural attractions on the one hand, and those sectors that support these tourism attractions, such as hospitality and transport, on the other.

1.3.2 South Africa's natural and cultural attractions

South Africa has such an abundance of natural and cultural attractions that it is almost impossible to describe them; this is also not the purpose of this book. Many books on these resources are readily available. What you, as a potential entrepreneur, need to know is what is meant by a natural tourist attraction and what is meant by a cultural tourist attraction. You need to know this so that you can make informed decisions when you decide to start a business and have to research the environment in which you are going to operate. Swarbrooke (1999) suggests that we categorise attractions into four types.

1. Features within the natural environment (here we can think of our wonderful national parks such as the Kruger National Park or natural features such as Table Mountain).
2. Human-made buildings, structures and sites that were designed for a purpose other than attracting visitors, but now attract substantial numbers of visitors who use them as leisure amenities. The best example of a famous site that was not built to attract tourists but that has become one of our major attractions is Robben Island.
3. Human-made buildings, structures and sites that are designed to attract visitors and are purpose-built to accommodate their needs, such as theme parks. While theme parks in South Africa are quite rare, other human-made structures such as Sun City and the Lost City resort fall within this category.
4. Special events. South Africa is becoming a popular venue for such events, such as the 2010 Soccer World Cup, cultural festivals such as the Klein Karoo Kunstefees and the Grahamstown Arts Festival, and many others such as the annual Tourism Indaba.

These natural and cultural attractions need to be supported by infrastructure, hospitality facilities and organisations supplying products and services to tourists, the two main sectors being the transport sector and the hospitality sector, which will be briefly discussed.

1.3.3 The transport sector in a nutshell

When we discuss transport from a tourism perspective, we must distinguish between:

- transport to and from a destination; and
- transport within a destination.

We must also add a category where the mode of transport may actually be the tourist 'destination', such as the Blue Train, Rovos Rail or a sea cruise. Transport to and from a destination provides the accessibility needed for a tourist to move from his/her home base (the tourist-generating area) to the destination of his/her choice (the tourist destination) and is exceptionally important for the growth of tourism in a destination. South Africa is regarded as a 'long-haul' destination. This means that people travelling from most parts of the world, such as the Americas, Europe, the Middle East and Asia, will travel in excess of ten hours to reach the destination. Short-haul travel is travel over short distances, such as within Europe from one country to another or within a country. South Africa, as a long-haul destination for most tourists, must promote its tourist product in such a way that tourists can spend some time in South Africa enjoying various sights, regions and experiences. Because South Africa is regarded as a long-haul destination, air capacity (i.e. the number of airlines flying into and out of the country) is extremely important, as this can be an important factor in the growth in the number of tourists or it can inhibit tourism to the country. Air capacity to a large extent determines the number of tourists that we receive. Most people must use air travel to reach South Africa, but of course there are other forms of transport as well, especially when we begin to look at transportation within the destination. Table 1.1 provides a broad categorisation of the various modes of passenger transport.

Table 1.1:   The passenger transport structure for tourism

Sector	Sub-sector	Example
Air	• Scheduled airlines (international and domestic)	SAA; kulula.com; 1time
	• Charter airlines	Million Air Charter
Road	Bus/coach: Scheduled	Greyhound
	Charter	Elwierda
	Tour operator	Springbok Atlas
	Cars: Private	Own car; 4x4
	Rental	Avis; Budget; Imperial; Tempest

	Motorbike	Britz Africa
	Vehicles used for:	
	Accommodation:	
	Motorhome, camper	Own caravan
Rail	Private	Rovos Rail; The Union Limited
	Public (Spoornet): Luxury	Blue Train
	Intercity	Trans-Natal
Water	Sea: Private sailing	Yachts
	Commercial	Group charters
	Cruising	Caribbean Cruises
Other	Cycling	Cycling tours
	Walking	Walking tours

a. Air transport

The airline industry has grown from infant to giant in 50 years. In 2004, the world's airlines carried 1,8 billion passengers with a forecast growth of 6% per year to 2008 (IATA, 2004). While growth has been healthy, airlines the world over experienced heavy financial losses in recent years, but are now slowly recovering. It was mostly the larger airlines that carried the highest volumes of passengers that suffered financially. It is of the utmost importance to have a stable and healthy air transportation industry, for without airline passengers, the tourist industry suffers greatly, as beds go unsold and attractions go unvisited. Because transportation is and will always be an essential ingredient in travel and tourism, the future of the airline industry continues to remain linked to the performance of the entire tourism industry.

Air transportation (this excludes privately owned aircraft) basically can be categorised under the following headings:

* scheduled airlines; and
* charter airlines.

Scheduled airlines have the following characteristics: convenient schedules that generally offer frequent and regular departures; good safety records with adherence to prescribed international standards of safety; and customer focused services for both leisure and business travellers. Scheduled airlines, particularly full service airlines, are also the most expensive mode of transportation. Due to increasing competition and declining yields in the air transport sector, the last few years have seen the introduction and growth of so-called low-cost airlines. In South Africa we have two low-cost carriers, namely kulula.com and 1time. 1time can be regarded as a true entrepreneurial enterprise (refer to the case study on page

120). These airlines, also sometimes known as no-frills airlines, have presented an alternative in the air transport market, especially for leisure travellers, who are very price conscious. These airlines have created a new market for air travel. Travellers that previously could not afford to fly to a destination are now able to buy air tickets rather than use surface transportation.

Business travellers generally prefer scheduled services, although the low cost airlines are now rapidly moving into the business travel market. For example, kulula.com has launched their Bizdeals product, which is specifically designed to meet the needs of business travellers who require the flexibility to be able to change or cancel a flight if necessary. Even though the company for which the business traveller works generally pays for the flight, which often means that the business traveller is less price sensitive, companies are now becoming more cost conscious and are managing their travel budgets more carefully. Holiday tourists are generally aware of price and have more time to shop around for the lowest prices and the best value for money because they plan their holidays well in advance, they do not need the same degree of flexibility.

South African Airways dominates the international routes to and from South Africa, with Nationwide operating flights into London as well, but there are various international carriers, such as British Airways, Lufthansa, Cathay Pacific, Air France, KLM, Virgin Atlantic and many others, that operate scheduled flights to southern Africa. Domestically, South African Airways dominates the market, but smaller carriers such as British Airways/Comair and Nationwide compete for a share of the local market, together with the two low-cost carriers. Regional airlines such as Interair, Royal Swazi Air, Air Botswana, Air Zimbabwe, Namibia Airlines and so forth also operate on the subcontinent.

While **charter airlines** are a popular form of travel for holidaymakers in overseas countries such as the United Kingdom and Europe, they are not generally a viable option for regular travel in South Africa, due to the relatively small flying public. One international charter company that operates out of South Africa is LTU. Charter airlines fly on routes where they can generate large numbers of passengers. They are not obliged to fly on a regular basis, but depend on mass tourism to fill their flights, which are pre-arranged to suit tourists' needs. They generally offer less in the way of services both in the air and on the ground, and in this way can offer much reduced fares compared to scheduled airlines. Due to the lack of regular air service in a number of African countries, *private aircraft charter companies* are more frequently used to fly into neighbouring and other African countries from South Africa. These aircraft usually carry from four to 18 passengers. Business executives and small groups generally charter these planes. They offer the advantages of convenience and flexibility to the users. Flights can be arranged to just about any destination at very short notice. With the expanding business opportunities in Africa, this mode of transport is popular among business executives. This service is primarily used by larger corporations whose managers need to travel quickly and suddenly to remote destinations not served by scheduled airlines (Lubbe, Bennett & Smuts, 1997).

Tel: (021) 936 1190   Fax:(021) 936 1189   E-mail:cpt@ltu.co.za

By courtesy of LTU

b. Road transport

Road transport has gained much ground in the past few decades. This can be ascribed to the improvement in the reliability of road transport and the relative cost, in line with the upgrading of roads and vehicle performance. Also, on low-density traffic routes, road transport is the only viable form of mechanical transport. Road transport, as opposed to all the other modes, has the potential to provide a door-to-door service, depending on the accessibility and efficiency of the existing road network, which makes it possible to reach areas over a wide geographical region.

Road transport can be subdivided into the following categories:

* private cars;
* rented cars;
* buses; and
* coaches or tour buses.

The **private car** accounts for most of the world's travel. Private car travel is likely to increase due to its convenience, flexibility and affordability. The national highway system significantly encourages holiday travel and especially long-distance travel. Tourists can drive from Johannesburg to Cape Town with the knowledge that a petrol station with rest rooms and shopping facilities is available approximately every 200 kilometres. This highway system must be kept in sound condition due to its increasing use, especially during peak periods, where capacity is stretched to the limit. People tend to favour travel by car. The main reason is its accessibility and flexibility. A car owner can leave from his/her doorstep at any time of the day and follow his/her own route to the destination of his/her choice with as many stopover points as necessary. Private car travellers are also more likely to be price sensitive. The cost of travel by car for three travellers to and from Cape Town is much lower per person than the price of a return air ticket. However, as distance increases, air travel becomes the main competitor for this industry, where speed, service and comfort must be weighed against price and accessibility of the car.

Rented cars have the same advantages as private cars, but they are much more expensive than private cars. They are very attractive to business travellers who are less sensitive to price, but insist on speed of service, reliability and a little more luxury. Two main categories of car hire companies can be identified:

- *large international companies* such as Avis, Budget and Imperial, boasting sophisticated reservation systems and multiple distribution points; and
- *smaller, local independent* hire companies such as Swan and Dolphin, which are more geographically focused.

In addition to this, companies such as CI Leisure Rentals, Leisure Mobiles and Campers Corner rent campers to tourists wishing to explore Southern Africa in this way. The country's climate greatly lends itself to this option. Rental cars are particularly popular on Mondays to Fridays amongst business travellers, while leisure travel represents the bulk of weekend rentals. Airport terminals are a major distribution point, thus making fly-drives a popular package.

Buses and coaches are an integral part of the tourism system. The motor coach industry is well suited for trips of 800km or less each way. Long-distance bus companies generally have comfortable seats, picture windows, rest rooms and even hostesses that serve passengers en route. There are a number of carriers that serve a national network: Greyhound, InterCape and Translux. Coaches provide a means of transport in rural areas where air and rail travel services are severely limited due to the sparse populations and geographical spread.

Intercity bus services are geared towards lower-income, price conscious, leisure travellers, visiting friends and relatives. Intercity bus services have shrunk to a minor transportation alternative because of increased car ownership and aggressive domestic airline pricing. Advocates for the bus industry believe that this form of transportation is well suited for shorter one-way trips. To distinguish between the terms 'bus' and 'coach' we can say that bus refers to intercity travel undertaken mainly by individuals on a point-to-point journey, while coach generally refers to inclusive-type tours created for groups of tourists exploring a region and all its attractions. Companies such as Springbok Atlas do tours of the regions, using coaches which generally include the services of a multilingual tour guide. Bus services, while equally as comfortable and luxurious as coaches, are offered for commuting between the major cities and towns in southern Africa.

Motsamai Travel and Tours

Motsamai Travel and Tours is a travel- and tourism-operating enterprise. Tours are conducted by qualified national tourist guides and are available right across South Africa. Standard tours are offered, as well as tours tailored to meet specific needs. The reservation office takes care of all flight, hotel and car hire bookings.

c. Rail transport

Rail travel in European and other countries forms a large part of tourist travel, with trains even being seen as competitors to airlines for short-haul travel. There are also a number of high-speed trains that make the effective travel time on certain routes for tourists more attractive than air travel over the same routes. Trains have also been designed to accommodate tourists and have facilities on board that make the train experience very comfortable. The most important

By courtesy of Rovos Rail

feature of rail travel in most established tourist destinations in Europe, the USA and Asia is that it is safe, has opportunities to view the countryside and is a comfortable form of travel. Tourists thus often plan their trips to include rail travel as an activity that can enhance their experience.

At the moment, inbound foreign tourists do not generally use rail travel in South Africa, as trains are perceived to be unsafe. This is particularly true for commuter travel within cities or for short distances. Intercity rail travel is used for people travelling between major cities and is mostly used by South Africans. The long distances between South African cities also make it difficult for trains to compete with cars and aircraft. However, train journeys are still popular in some market segments. Trains in South Africa that are very popular amongst foreign visitors are the luxury trains such as the Blue Train and Rovos Rail, with Rovos Rail being an excellent example of entrepreneurial skill and perseverance (refer to the case study on page 123). These trains can be considered tourist attractions in themselves and many tourists will make these journeys the focal point of their tourism experience in South Africa. Other rail trips that are designed for tourists rather than point-to-point travel are the scenic train trips, which can be combined with other tourist activities such as visits to game reserves. In this regard, we can highlight trains such as the Outeniqua Express and trains from Pretoria to Cullinan for day trips.

The author of a paper delivered at the Africa Rail 2002 conference held at Midrand in 2002 makes a number of interesting suggestions as to how rail travel can be exploited for tourism purposes. He says that the potential for tourism in a railway context should not be confined to steam locomotives only. South Africa has always been in the forefront of locomotive developments. South Africa's rich railway heritage includes many other achievements that are potentially 'marketable' to overseas visitors. Some of them include the following.

1 The Natal Government Railways (NGR) was among the first in the world to introduce the 4-8-2-steam loco wheel arrangement.
2 NGR also took the worldwide lead in 1887 with steam locomotives with ten driving wheels.
3 NGR was one of the first railways to run 1 000-ton trains (transporting coal for export from the Natal midlands to Durban), using the locomotives mentioned above.
4 In 1924, South African Railways (SAR) introduced the 1E electric locomotive, which for several years was the most numerous type of electric loco in the world (172 locos). Since then, the class 6E/6EI (with over 1 000 examples) has become one of the most numerous types.
5 From 1936 to 1955, the line between Durban and Volksrust was the longest electrified stretch of railway in the world (500 km).
6 According to the *Guinness Book of Records*, SAR holds the record for the longest train in the world (7 km – 71 000 tons).
7 SAR operated the largest steam locomotives on 3'6" and 2'0" gauge respectively. It used more Garratt-type locomotives than any other railway, as well as more condensing-type locos.

8 The Alfred Country Railway (2'0" gauge) between Port Shepstone and Harding has operated some of the heaviest trains on that gauge (845 tons), climbing gradients of 1 in 40 in the process. The longest 2'0" gauge line in the world runs from Port Elizabeth to Avontuur (277 km).

9 The highest speed on 3'6" gauge (245 km/h) has been achieved in South Africa. It has also been in the forefront of developments in electric traction and dual-power (electro-diesel) technology.

d. Water transportation

This industry is at present the fastest-growing part of the local tourist industry. Cruising in South Africa is 'booming', with monthly figures for 2005 greatly surpassing comparable figures for 2004 (Berger, 2005:5). According to industry experts, innovative shore destinations are the main trend for 2005. Interesting combinations of cruising and touring are increasingly appearing. One example is where passengers can take a cruise and use the 4x4 vehicle on board for touring onshore.

By courtesy of Andrew Weir Shipping

Cruise lines are expanding their fleets, as more and more passengers want to travel by cruise liner. Cruises are actually floating resorts providing point-to-point transportation. The industry enjoys a very high level of passenger satisfaction. The average length of a cruise has dropped to three- and five-day cruises with a shift towards a younger market, including families with children. In the South African market, a number of cruising agents can be found (such as Starlight Cruises and Orient Lines). These agents arrange for a large number of cruises to and from a variety of very popular destinations.

Smaller cruising operations with strong individual entrepreneurial characteristics have also proved to be very successful, one of which is Dyer Island Cruises (refer to the case study on page 124).

1.3.4 The hospitality sector

The supply of tourism products basically involves how the various components of the tourist product are placed at the disposal of the tourist. From our discussion above we know that these suppliers can be classified under the following headings:

- **attractions** (this can be seen as the draw card to a destination, i.e. the main reason why a tourist will visit a specific destination);
- **transport** (the various modes of transport to allow tourist access to all these attractions); and
- **hospitality** (the accommodation, food service and entertainment components during the journey phase and at the destination).

As far as hospitality is concerned, this is where a tourist will be looking at the following:

- appropriate forms of accommodation;
- different types of food service provisioning;
- entertainment and leisure activities; and
- gaming.

The suppliers of hospitality products, be it accommodation, food service, entertainment or gaming, must be well located in relation to the other components of the tourism product.

The suppliers of accommodation services in South Africa vary from privately owned organisations to large hotel chain groups or consortiums. Some of the largest hotel groups in South Africa are the Sun International Group, Southern Sun and Protea Hotels. Other forms of accommodation include:

- **guesthouses or pensions** – providing a more personal touch and often a true 'African' touch;

- **hostels** (usually for young people) – providing basic, cheap accommodation;
- **motels** – next to roads and with plentiful parking space;
- **game lodges**; and
- **timeshare accommodation** – becoming more popular in South Africa, where the interchange of timeshare accommodation can be made throughout the world.

The Village Boiketlo Guesthouse
Owner: Sheila Mareka
The Village Boiketlo Guesthouse is the only guesthouse in Bloemfontein that offers the true African touch. The 15 rooms are decorated using the 'Big Five' motif and the guesthouse also offers African cultural dances and meals.

The food services industry is strongly linked to the accommodation sector and includes eating and drinking places ranging from restaurants, fast food outlets and coffee shops to roadside food outlets and shebeens.

Restaurants that are becomingly increasingly popular in the tourism industry, particularly for foreign inbound tourists, are the traditional restaurants, one of which is the Sakhumzi Restaurant in Johannesburg, which was selected as a finalist by SA Tourism in their ETEYA Awards for Tourism Entrepreneurs (refer to the case study on page 125).

Leisure activities involve the activities of people engaging in constructive and personally pleasurable use of leisure time and may include passive or active participation in individual or group sports, cultural functions, natural and human history appreciation, non-formal education and sightseeing. These activities are often at the core of the tourism experience.

Gambling in South Africa has flourished against all odds since the first legislation on gaming was enacted 200 years ago. Gambling in the early days was not for recreation. Many newly created millionaires on the diamond and gold fields played deadly serious games and sometimes saw their fortunes wiped out after prolonged card games.

Although gambling legislation dates back to 1789, to the times of the Dutch East India Company, hard gambling originated on the mines. The discovery of diamonds attracted many inveterate gamblers to South Africa. The early diggers in Kimberley gambled with cards, billiards, dominoes and dice, with stakes of thousands of pounds at a time. Where Kimberley left off, Johannesburg took over. Early Johannesburg hotels catered firstly for the gamblers' needs, before seeing to the comfort of the guests. Gaming has evolved in South Africa as well as internationally from an illegal activity to a major growth industry. In various jurisdictions throughout the world, a wide variety of gaming industries have been created for the purpose of stimulating tourism, bolstering regional or local economies, creating jobs and employment opportunities, and generating tax revenues.

With the institution of the new gambling legislation in South Africa and the opening of 40 new casinos, the gambling environment is becoming very competitive. Established casinos, in the previously 'zoned' homelands, are losing their stronghold on gambling as a result of easier entrance to the market and even Sun International, previously so favoured, has to apply for the right to offer gambling facilities.

1.4   LINKING SUPPLY AND DEMAND

Apart from the physical accessibility of a destination, which is made possible through transport, a destination's 'accessibility' is also dependent on how a tourist actually arranges his/her trip and fulfils a number of essential tasks prior to departure. Once a tourist decides he/she wants to go on holiday, the first decision he/she makes is where he/she would like to go. Awareness of the attractiveness of a destination puts that destination on his/her list of possibilities. Once he/she has decided on the destination, certain arrangements and documents must be in place before departure. These can include correct entry documentation, transport arrangements, advance reservations, ticketing and currency. All these activities fall within the so-called **distribution system** in tourism.

Simply put, the distribution system makes the supply side of tourism available and accessible to the demand side. Because tourism is an intangible product, **information** is the only thing on which potential tourists can base their decisions and make their arrangements. Before we discuss the tourism distribution system, we need therefore to highlight the importance of information in the tourism industry.

Consider when you plan a holiday. Probably the most important consideration is the money that it will cost. You may spend evenings browsing the Internet or looking through brochures for information on the region you wish to visit. You also take time to find out what the weather will be like, what you can do at the destination and what you will need to make your holiday the best ever. The investment you make in terms of time and money in planning and taking your holiday is considerable. You want good, accurate and up-to-date information to make it all worthwhile. Even if you are going on a business trip and your company is investing the money, you still want to know that the information you have is correct so that your trip can run smoothly and time and effort is not wasted because of incorrect information. For example, if you want to stay in a hotel close to your business meetings, you want to be able to rely on the information you have obtained that says that the hotel is situated where you require it. Remember we said that a tourist product cannot be returned, exchanged or even refunded in most cases and a travel experience that has gone wrong is an experience lost forever. The amount and complexity of information needed by tourists and provided by industry is best described by O'Connor (1999:2) as follows:

Even the simplest trip means trying to match the expectations of diverse travellers to the bewildering array of choices and options provided by millions of tourism suppliers, each trying to differentiate themselves from their competitors. Given that millions of people travel every day, it can be seen that the communication of accurate, current and relevant information is essential to the efficient operation of the tourism industry.

Leisure and business tourists need information *before* and *during* a trip to make the investment in time and money worthwhile. The tourism product is an intangible and perishable service. People perform this service while you are experiencing it (the air hostess on an airline, the receptionist or waiter in a hotel or the tour guide on a tour). You cannot pre-test this service before buying it and you cannot return it if it goes wrong. This is why, in tourism, we generally only have one chance to get it right, otherwise we lose our customers very quickly. Compare a tourism service to a manufactured product such as a stove – before you buy it, you can pre-test it; once you decide to buy, you can have it packaged and leave with it; and if it is faulty, you can return it to have it repaired or replaced. This is not possible in tourism. Tourists have to rely on information to make their travel choices. The distribution system provides this information and makes the tourism service accessible and available to tourists.

There are basically four components in the tourism distribution system. The first component is made up of the **suppliers** of tourism services (the hotels, airlines, attractions and other service providers). When suppliers use their own sales outlets, call centres, the Internet and other booking tools, they can achieve *direct distribution. Indirect distribution* is achieved through the use of intermediaries. Figure 1.3, on page 22, shows the various links and organisations in the distribution system. The role of travel suppliers is to provide travel related services to consumers. They rely on the **distribution** of information through **distributors**, the second component of the system, to consumers. The distributors have the capacity to store vast amounts of information on all the products and services available worldwide in tourism, (from airline seats to hotel rooms, sightseeing tours and much more). Global distribution systems such as Galileo and Amadeus, are used mainly by travel intermediaries and store fairly standardised information on airline seats, large hotel chains, car rental companies and so on. Destination management systems, also distributors, generally store information on destinations and regions where the information has a far richer and varied content than the information generally stored on global distribution systems. This information includes small enterprises such as guest houses, sightseeing attractions such as museums and local events, transport schedules and routes within a region and interesting local information. Think of South Africa and its provinces: how would you find out more about what is available for tourists in these regions?

Access the websites provided below and find out the following:

1. What are the most popular places to visit in the region?
2. What advice does the website give on where to stay and what to do?
3. When are the best times to visit the region?
4. How can tourists book their trips to the region?

www.tourismnorthwest.co.za; www.kzn.org.za; www.gauteng.net

The third component is made up of **travel intermediaries** such as tour wholesalers and travel agents. Travel agents have traditionally been the dominant sales channel for the airline and tour operating companies. Suppliers used to pay travel agents a commission but in recent years this commission has been greatly reduced and travel agents are now collecting a service fee from customers. This has meant that customers are looking for greater value for money and are also doing more research into different channels such as the Internet for travel information and bookings. Travel agents have become more specialised and there has been a clear distinction in serving the leisure and business markets. The business travel market consists of independent business travellers who may still make use of travel agents, and so-called corporate travellers who make use of the services of *travel management companies* (TMCs) appointed by their companies especially to handle all the travel of that particular company. The TMC still does travel reservations, issues tickets, consults with corporate travellers on their travel requirements and produces itineraries, as any travel agent does but will also provide the company with accurate management information on their travel patterns and expenditure, assist with travel policy formulation and implementation, and negotiate discounts with travel supplies. An intermediary that serves the leisure market is the *tour wholesaler*. The tour wholesaler produces inclusive or package tours consisting of the different components of the tourism product, such as transportation, accommodation and sightseeing and generally sells these via the travel agent to the consumer who is interested in going on a pre-arranged tour. Tour wholesalers range from large organisations such as Thompsons Tours to small, niche-market-oriented tour wholesalers. Travel intermediaries such as travel agents and tour wholesalers have also established their own websites and effectively become 'virtual travel offices', providing the same services as they do 'off-line' (*traditionally*) but allowing the customer to access the travel agency from his/her office or home or even on his/her laptop. The final component of the distribution system consists of **customers**, segmented into business and leisure tourists.

Asambe opens Soweto travel agency
Siza Nkuta has opened her Soweto-based travel agency, Siza's Travel, a non-IATA agency, which falls under the Asambe umbrella. Asambe (which means 'let's go') is a travel and leisure savings club aimed at making domestic and international tourism more affordable to

previously disadvantaged people. The organisation establishes partnerships with members like Siza to assist in selling travel and to recruit members for the savings club.

Siza started recruiting members for Asambe while she was still working as a cashier for Pick 'n Pay. When she had recruited more than 350 members, Asambe decided to help her establish her own agency. The organisation gave her in-house training, which mainly consisted of product and broader travel and tourism training, allowing her to advise tourists about destinations in South Africa and abroad. For all bookings, she contacts Asambe.

Asambe's executive director and chairman, Sakhiwo Tshabalala, explained that Asambe provides assistance to new agency owners with regard to set-up costs, as well as a small monthly amount to cover basic overheads. Agency owners make money on the handling fees and commissions.

Two more agencies are due to be launched this year in Rustenburg and Tembisa, according to Sakhiwo. Minister of Environmental Affairs and Tourism Marthinus van Schalkwyk has said: 'Siza Nkuta is an example to all South Africans. Despite having started her career as a cashier at a supermarket, her hard work, dedication, perseverance and the support of companies such as Asambe Investment Holdings have shown that everyone in South Africa can reap the benefits of tourism.' Dorine Berger, *Travel News Weekly*, 1863, 4 May 2005, p. 2

To summarise, **suppliers** may be broadly defined as any producer who has products or services to sell. **Distributors** store and disseminate information, and **intermediaries** may be described as any third party or organisation between the producer and consumer that facilitates purchases by transferring the service to the buyer and also providing sales revenue to the producer. **Customers** may be defined as people who have the need for, want and are able and willing to buy a product or service. Figure 1.3 provides a comprehensive view of the tourism distribution system and we can see that there are a number of channels available to tourists when they want to find information and book their trips. As can be seen from Figure 1.3, travel intermediaries such as travel agents and tour wholesalers form important components of the distribution system, but they are not the only links between the supplier and the buyer. The number of links may vary from simple distribution links where the supplier sells directly to the customer, called **direct distribution**, to complex distribution links involving several layers of members such as retail travel agents and tour wholesalers/operators, this is called **indirect distribution**. As you can see in Figure 1.3, some new channels are also emerging. These include kiosks, personal digital assistants and interactive TV. Some of these channels are already being used quite extensively in some countries such as the United Kingdom and are slowly starting to emerge in South Africa.

We have discussed tourism from the viewpoint of the demand for tourism (types of tourists and tourist flows) and the supply of tourism (the attractions of a destination and the organisations such as transport and accommodation establishments that serve the tourist's needs). We have also discussed how supply and demand are linked through distribution, explained the importance

MODEL FOR TRAVEL DISTRIBUTION

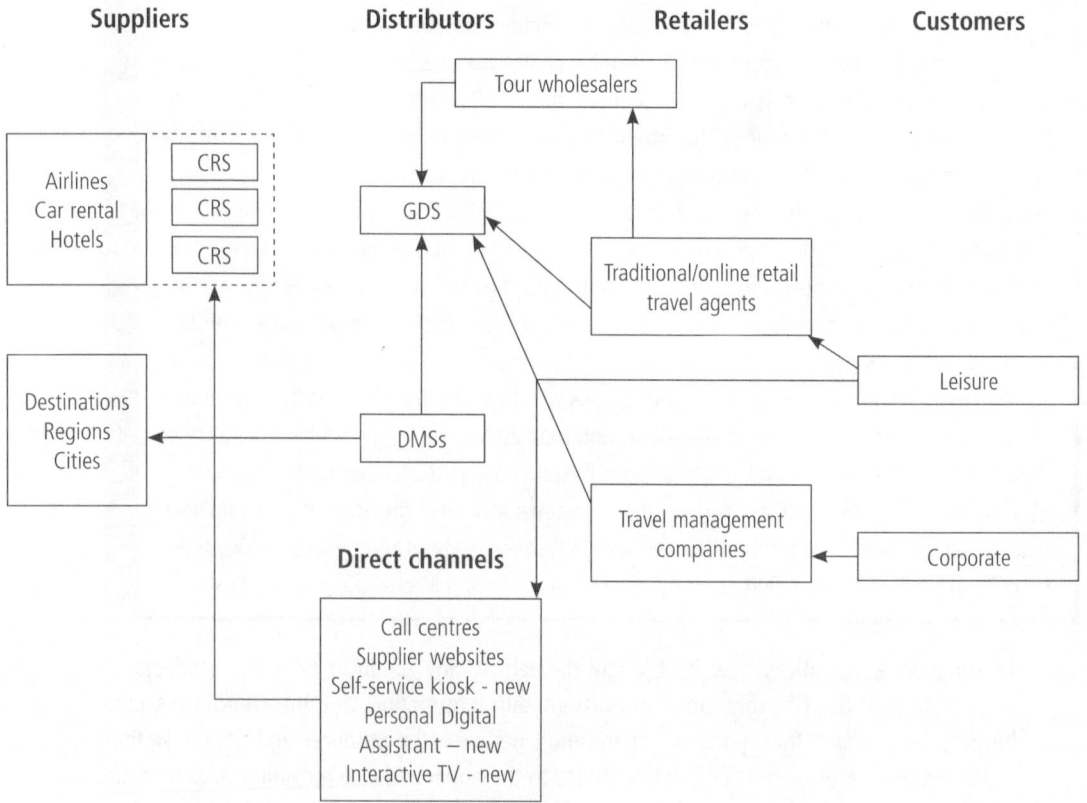

Suppliers	Distributors	Retailers	Customers

```
                              Tour wholesalers

   Airlines    CRS
   Car rental  CRS        GDS
   Hotels      CRS                      Traditional/online retail
                                              travel agents

                                                                    Leisure

   Destinations
   Regions            DMSs
   Cities
                                          Travel management
                 Direct channels              companies            Corporate

                     Call centres
                  Supplier websites
                Self-service kiosk - new
                   Personal Digital
                   Assistrant – new
                  Interactive TV - new
```

Figure 1.3   Current tourism distribution model

of information in the tourism industry and shown which organisations make the tourist product available and accessible to the tourist. Finally, we must look at the broader environment in which tourism operates, as this environment also affects the whole tourism system.

1.5   THE MACRO-ENVIRONMENT

Events in the broader environment (the so-called **macro-environment**) have always had an impact on if, how and where people will travel. These events include everything from political statements by leaders of countries (Zimbabwe is a good example of the negative impact on tourism of political statements made by its leader) and natural disasters such as the tsunami of 26 December 2004, to terrorist attacks (the World Trade Center in the USA, and Egypt, Kenya, Thailand and many more countries that have been struck by terrorism), health issues (severe acute respiratory syndrome or SARS, AIDS, malaria), and the state of the economies of countries (South Africa has felt a decline in tourism as a result of the strong rand). Not only have religious, political, health and economic issues had an impact on the growth or decline of tourism in different countries, but developments in technology, transport, and local and global business have also influenced the way in which people travel.

The WTTC states: 'History shows that the travel and tourism industry is particularly vulnerable to severe business downturns during periods of terrorism, political uncertainty, military conflict and health-related crises.' As a result of the impact of the terrorist attacks in the USA on 11 September 2001, SARS, the crisis in Iraq, global terrorism and the state of the economies of various countries, there was worldwide stagnation in the growth of tourism between 2000 and 2003, as is shown in Figure 1.4.

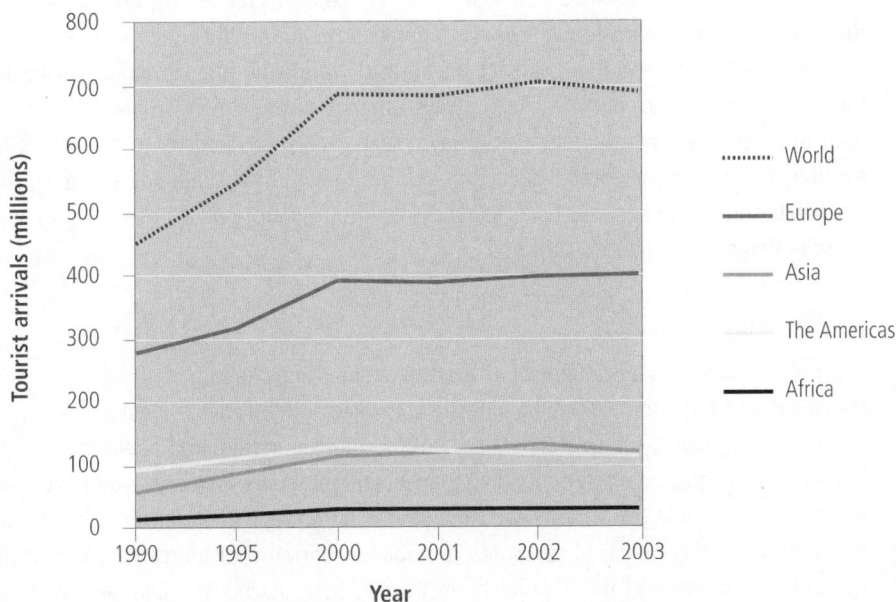

Figure 1.4   International tourist arrivals, 1990–2003

Source: Consolidated figures from the WTTC (2005)

The WTO says the following about 2004: 'Global tourism saw a spectacular rebound in 2004 … with arrivals up 10% last year after prolonged stagnation. The 10% jump in arrivals to 760 million was the highest rise since 1984.' Asia and the Pacific grew by 29%, the Middle East by 20%, while Africa and Europe were below world average, but still better than previous results. Countries in the euro zone, Australia, Canada, New Zealand and South Africa were affected by exchange rates (*WTO Winter Barometer Report*, 2005).

But not only events affect tourism; people change as well. Tourists have changed in the way in which they travel and what they want to do. More people are travelling, because travel is becoming more affordable with the advent of 'low-cost' airlines, accommodation, car rental and other tourism services, as well as the increase in disposable income. In South Africa, we are seeing a strong emerging market – a market that was previously ignored by tourism suppliers. Not only are those people that were disadvantaged under the apartheid system starting to discover the joys of travelling as tourists, but they themselves are emerging as successful tourism entrepreneurs, starting businesses in rural areas and 'townships' that provide authentic African tourism experiences, or in cities providing travel and tourism services for travellers in general.

Lifestyles and consumer demands are changing, and people are becoming more demanding, but at the same there is an increase in environmental awareness, causing destinations to re-look at the sustainability of their natural habitats. More and more people are travelling as a result of an increase in their disposable incomes, but concerns for security are affecting where they are going, with more people looking at domestic holidays. While the macro-environment undoubtedly has an enormous impact on tourism worldwide and on individual countries, tourism managers and marketers will always attempt to use the environment to stimulate tourism to grow effectively. They will always make predictions and try to control, as far as possible, these environmental impacts. Through destination marketing, policy and legislation, the establishment of organisations to represent the tourism industry research, as well as coordination of the system is achieved.

1.6 CONCLUSION

This first chapter introduces tourism as a system comprising the tourist, the tourism industry, the way in which the tourist and the industry are linked and the environment in which tourism operates. It highlights the interdependency of the tourism system and how each role-player has a significant part to play. For budding tourism entrepreneurs, it creates a broad foundation for the understanding of tourism and how you as an entrepreneur can fit into the system. We have used some practical cases and examples to show what tourism entrepreneurs are currently doing. We end this chapter by explaining how the book is laid out, so that as a potential tourism entrepreneur, you can begin to generate ideas, and plan and launch your small business in this vibrant industry.

1.7 THE AIM AND STRUCTURE OF THIS BOOK

With this book, we aim to provide you, as a budding tourism entrepreneur or student studying business management and tourism, with the knowledge and skills to start and manage your own small business. We take you through a process of understanding what tourism and the tourism industry is all about and where you (the entrepreneur) fit into the industry. The book allows you to move from the idea stage to the writing of a business plan and prepares you for the processes of financing your venture, assessing the environment and market, identifying marketing opportunities, highlighting the risks involved and planning the financial management of your business. The book also provides a wealth of resources that can be accessed, from legal to business networking opportunities. Finally, it contributes to your understanding of how a business should be managed to achieve success.

The book is structured as follows:

In chapter 1, we give a broad overview of what tourism is.

In chapter 2, we look at the whole question of creativity and opportunity recognition by defining what creativity is, explaining the blocks to creativity, the process of creative thinking, how to use creativity in tourism, idea generation for tourism entrepreneurs, identifying opportunities and, finally, how to establish a sustainable competitive advantage.

In chapter 3, we discuss starting your own business and the reasons for wanting to do so. We identify those things that influence the start-up decision, such as location, infrastructure and where the new service or product fits into the product life cycle.

Chapter 4 concentrates on the business plan, beginning with the reasons why planning is needed and why a business plan is so important. We discuss the elements of the business plan and how it should be presented and we also look at some reasons why business plans sometimes fail.

Chapter 5 takes a look at the resources needed when starting a business, examines how to assemble the resources and get essential information, and expands on the human and financial resources required in a new business.

The last chapter, chapter 6, focuses on managing the growth of the new venture and the essential skills required for entrepreneurs to manage their businesses effectively. Other aspects that are covered relate to marketing the venture, resources development and management, financial control and record-keeping, strategic planning skills, networking and support, customer service, time management, ethical behaviour and quality management. In the unlikely event of your experiencing a worst-case scenario, we give some advice on ending your venture.

2 Creativity and Opportunity Recognition

Melodi Botha

Once you have worked through this chapter, you should be able to:

☞ Define and understand creativity

☞ Understand why creative skills are important for entrepreneurs

☞ Use the process of creative thinking to improve your entrepreneurial skills

☞ Know the difference between an opportunity and an idea

☞ Understand the criteria that one can use to assess venture opportunities

☞ Know how to protect your products or services

☞ Establish a sustainable competitive advantage for your business

2.1 INTRODUCTION

Why are some entrepreneurs more successful than others? One of the primary driving forces of successful entrepreneurs is found in their ability to be creative. Creative behaviour and thinking lead to innovative actions and processes. Creativity and innovation should form part of your life when you are starting and running your own tourism business. It is especially important to realise that in the tourism industry, you should always think of new and innovative ways to serve and satisfy your customers. It is said that everyone is creative, but some people just exploit their creative flair more than others. Luckily, creativity is something that can be developed and practised. This chapter will help you to improve your creative skills and enable you to use your creative problem-solving ability more effectively. This section of the book will also identify the barriers to creativity that you must be aware of when starting or running your own business. Opportunities within the tourism industry are also identified, as well as ways to exploit and protect those opportunities.

2.2 DEFINING CREATIVITY

According to Nieman, Hough and Nieuwenhuizen (2003:48), there are more than 450 definitions of creativity, which have been developed over the last hundred years.

Couger (1995:14) defined creativity extensively and formulated it in the sense of being able to solve definite problems. His generally accepted definition contains the following conditions.

- The product of creativity is firstly the product or result of a thinking process. This product or idea should have novelty as its defining characteristic and should create value (i.e. the brain is uniquely utilised in the thinking process and the result is supposed to create a useful item).
- This thinking process is usually unconventional, meaning that previously accepted ideas or concepts are normally rejected or modified.
- The thinking process is supported by performance motivation and is mostly time- and energy-consuming.
- The initial problem is normally vague and unstructured. A definition of the problem is thus integrated as a key part of the thinking process – i.e. the thinking process actually defines the problem clearly. And when you know exactly what the problem is, solving it is much easier. It is important to realise how creativity and innovation can play a role in entrepreneurship. Creativity in entrepreneurship is recognising ideas that can become entrepreneurial opportunities. This stems from a capacity to see what others do not.

Let's refer to the example of 'Cook-up with Kamamma' to illustrate how creativity can be integrated into a business.

'Cook-up with Kamamma' is an exciting, participative and interactive cuisine experience, whereby 'Kamammas' (community matriarchs and entrepreneurs) teach visitors their culinary secrets at community restaurants on all the major tourist routes in South Africa. They not only serve truly South African cuisine, but also teach visitors how to make the dishes that they serve. The person who invented the idea therefore took an ordinary everyday skill (the ability to cook traditional dishes, which many people possess) and turned it into an entrepreneurial opportunity.

Being creative means that you are always creating new things and thinking of better ways of doing things. You are always questioning and striving to improve current products or uses of products/services.

2.3   BLOCKS TO CREATIVITY

The following blocks are normally seen as barriers or obstacles to thinking and acting creatively. These blocks can influence many entrepreneurial and business tasks that you as a tourism entrepreneur are supposed to carry out.

2.3.1 Environmental barriers

In this context, we look at social, economic and physical environments, and how they can hinder creativity.

- *Social environment:* This is typically the environment in which we are frightened to do anything different from the norm, because we do not want to be seen as being different or weird. In many South African cultures, risk-taking is not allowed and children are not encouraged to think for themselves; in other words, they do not get opportunities to live out their creativity. Those people who specialise in creative behaviour often suggest that children are the most creative human beings of all. We can learn a lot from them, yet we do not give them freedom to express themselves!
- *Economic environment:* This block results from the perception that if you do not have a lot of money, you can't be creative; in other words, no financial support is available for the development of new products.
- *Physical:* Routine can be seen as a block in the physical environment, because everything in life usually happens in some or other routine. The result is that we start to believe that something can only be done according to this conventional, routine way of doing things, and so we find it difficult to think of doing something in a new or different way. Have you ever tried travelling to work/school/university by following a different route to the one that you normally follow? You might find it very interesting and see things you have never seen before!

2.3.2 Cultural barriers

South Africa is an incredibly diverse country – we have more than 12 different cultural groups, each with its own traditions and cultures. But unfortunately, cultural attitudes can be a barrier to creativity. For example, in some cultures it is believed that women cannot be creative, let alone start their own businesses, and that they are only there to look after the children, prepare food, and take care of other household responsibilities. (But even this can be turned into an opportunity – as we have seen, Cook-up with Kamamma is an excellent example.)

2.3.3 Perceptual barriers

Some people believe that they are not creative and nothing can be done to improve their creativity skills. As a result, they tend to look at problems by only seeing the negative side and only formulating the obvious solution.

A key part of this process is having false assumptions about yourself; for example, when you believe that you are not creative and cannot become creative. If you see yourself in this way, it is obviously extremely unlikely that you will think any creative thoughts.

Habits are part of the barrier here; for example:

- believing that there is only one right answer;
- looking at a problem in isolation;
- always following the rules; and
- indulging in negative thinking.

2.3.4 The entrepreneur's attitude and emotions

Being a successful entrepreneur has a lot to do with your attitude and behaviour. In 1899,mthe director of the United States Patent Office, Charles Duell, stated that: 'Everything that can be invented has been invented.' Oh, was he wrong!! Entrepreneurs are still inventing and coming up with new ways of improving current products and services every day. If they had all had Duell's attitude, nothing would have been invented since 1899!

You have to think, believe and act creatively if you want to be creative. Thomas Edison was a person with a very positive attitude and also the person who invented the light bulb. He was very creative and held 1 093 patents.

- He knew 1 800 ways *not* to build a light bulb. This means that he was prepared to make endless mistakes until he got the formula for success right. And he never allowed himself to be downhearted while he was making all those mistakes.
- He kept a notebook so he could cross-fertilize ideas and techniques, and record observations. This meant that he could *learn from his mistakes*. Making a mistake is useless unless you can learn something from it. But if you are prepared to learn from it, it can be one of the most valuable things that you ever experience.

2.4 THE PROCESS OF CREATIVE THINKING

According to Nieman, Hough and Niewenhuizen (2003:47), creative behaviour and thinking lead to innovative actions and processes. Consider the most successful entrepreneurs on a global level. They have all discovered or invented new products, services or processes. Some of them only changed existing or conventional things or services into new ones. All of these actions are the result of intense creativity, which is a unique entrepreneurial skill.

The invention of drive-through restaurants is an excellent example. The business remains a restaurant offering the same food that it would normally serve, but customers can now order it at a window attached to the restaurant while sitting in their cars! It is an already-existing concept that has been changed or adapted to cater for new circumstances – the busy lives of modern people and the way the car has come to dominate our lives.

How do you get into shape for creative thinking? Basically, you must learn how creativity works, and then you must practise it. According to Mauzy and Harriman (2003:13) the following are necessary to help you to begin exercising your creativity.

- Motivation

  You have to be motivated to be creative and that is something that has to come from within yourself. Motivation also forms part of overcoming the blocks to creativity that we mentioned earlier in this chapter.

- Curiosity and fear

  It is good to be curious about what you might find when being creative and acting differently. Entrepreneurs are always aware of fear because it spells risks, and risks are part of the unknown. But being creative is a process of discovering the unknown, so you have to be prepared to take risks.

- Breaking and making connections to form new ideas

  It is important to be aware of the sources where you can find new ideas, as illustrated in section 2.6, below.

- Climate

  The climate within a business must be ideal for creativity to flare up. Usually, when an entrepreneur encourages change and innovation within his/her business, it is much easier for everyone concerned to be creative.

- Evaluation

  It is always important to evaluate what you have learned and how creativity has helped you in a specific situation. You will then be able to understand what happened and how it happened, and will therefore be more likely be able to do something similar next time. This will help get you into the habit of being creative.

- Perseverance

  Creativity means continuing to adjust and improve on your ideas. We have seen that Thomas Edison tried 1 801 times before he built the light bulb as we know it today. An entrepreneur cannot be successful if he/she does not adapt to changing customer needs. You need creativity to do so, but you also need perserverance, as circumstances are changing all the time, and you must be prepared to adapt more or less continuously.

2.5   USING CREATIVITY IN THE TOURISM INDUSTRY

Saayman and Saayman (1999:3) report that the South African tourism market has changed, and that creative people within the tourism industry have accepted and exploited this new paradigm by creating new products. Visits to townships and cultural villages, viewing of traditional dancing and experiencing a shebeen, to name but a few examples, have gained popularity.

Wandie's Place in Soweto has become a world-famous tourist site in South Africa. The clientele is among the most prestigious anywhere in the world – numerous heads of state, particularly African ones, have enjoyed a meal and a few drinks there, as have many ambassadors and celebrities. BUT Wandie's has not always been a thriving restaurant patronised by the rich and famous. Wandi Ndaba started operating an illegal shebeen from his house in 1981. Without a licence and in constant fear of police raids, he struggled through the next decade, relying on the loyalty of his regular clientele. In 1991, the shebeen was finally licensed, ushering in a new, prosperous phase in its history. While many shebeens stuck to the sale of liquor, Wandi carved a niche for himself by selling prepared food, initially offering fish and T-bone steak to his customers. With time, the business developed into a proper restaurant, complete with a menu and customer service, and appealing to the emergent local middle class. Impressed by the service offered at the venue, regular clients started inviting curious whites to go with them, mainly their colleagues from work who wanted some township experience. The Wine Foundation was the first to host a function of 60 white farmers in 1993 and this put Wandie's on the map. The restaurant also plays host to Frank Opperman (Ouboet in the television programme *Orkney Snork Nie*) and overseas luminaries such as Richard Branson, the CEO of Virgin Airlines; Evander Holyfield; Jesse Jackson; and Quincy Jones. Today, Wandie's hosts about 100 tourists a day – so if you don't book quite far ahead of time, you won't get a place at Wandie's.

The new tourists' different approach creates a demand for new products. Entrepreneurs in small, medium and micro-enterprises (SMMEs) within the tourism industry are dependent on major tourism developments, and must adapt creatively to these developments.

Koh (1996:30) defines tourism entrepreneurship as activities related to creating and operating a legal tourist enterprise. 'Legal enterprise' refers to a business that has been registered, operates on a profitable basis and seeks to satisfy the needs of tourists and visitors. Such enterprises include, among others, hotels, guesthouses, travel agencies and tour operators. Entrepreneurship and tourism can be seen as complementing each other in striving towards the mutual goal of generating employment opportunities in South Africa.

There are many opportunities that arise for entrepreneurs within the tourism industry in South Africa.

- The accommodation sector of the industry is growing fast – especially the development and operation of camping grounds, caravan parks, game parks, holiday camps, hotels, motels, chalets, bed-and-breakfast establishments and guesthouses. The guesthouse sector in South Africa has grown considerably over the past five years and indications are that this growth will be maintained in the near future. For example, Lolo's Guest House, situated in Diepkloof extension, Soweto, offers an exclusive township experience. The guesthouse has five bedrooms, four en suite, including a family room. The conference facilities can accommodate approximately 40 people. Lolo's is a bed-and-breakfast establishment, offers African cuisine dinners on request and has a three-star rating.

- The transport industry also holds many opportunities for potential entrepreneurs. In becoming a tour operator, the entrepreneur can package tours and then make use of other entrepreneurs for providing support services such as transporting people.
- Human-made attractions, for example, monuments, theme parks, waterfront developments, zoos, parks, game reserves, and wedding and conference venues, have also become a popular entrepreneurial activity. For example, Black Tie in Brooklyn, Pretoria is a one-stop wedding shop. Here you will find information about venues, flowers, candles, wedding gowns and even hair and make-up specialists. Black Tie has combined all of these services to give a bride a one-stop experience and provides the ultimate in convenience.

2.6   IDEA GENERATION AND IDENTIFICATION FOR TOURISM ENTREPRENEURS

Ideas are generated from various sources, some of which are discussed below.

- **From skills, expertise and aptitude:** Hopefully this chapter will inspire you to come up with new and innovative ideas. The more creative exercises you do, the more you will stimulate creativity within yourself.

> {?} Ask yourself: 'What am I good at?' and start from there.

- **From common needs:** Ideas are generated from needs that arise; for example, the invention of the microwave oven. People wanted something that could save them time and heat up their food quickly.

> {?} Ask yourself: 'What do I want but find difficult to get hold of?'

- **From existing situations:** There may be something out there that has been bothering you for a long time and you have been asking yourself the question: 'Why don't they do it this way or that way?' For example, Santawani Lodge found a creative way of solving the unemployment problem. During the 1990s, when large concession areas in the North-West District of Botswana were re-assessed and put out for tender, the Sankuyo community won the tender to manage the wildlife management areas that make up the bulk of the southern land boundary of the Moremi Game Reserve. In 2003, the community made the landmark decision to refurbish and manage the existing Santawani Lodge themselves, rather than hand the project over to be managed by a large tourism organisation. This means that the community directly benefits whether the customer books a fully inclusive safari, or simply buys a bundle of firewood. (Consult Santawani's website on www. santawani.com for further information.)
- **From everyday problems:** Maybe there is something that bothers you at your university, school or work and you can find a creative way of solving that problem.
- **From customers and consumers:** Your customers are often the best source to generate new ideas, because they are the ones that you have to satisfy. Make sure you are constantly busy with market research and questioning customers. They may plant a seed for a new

idea. This is in fact why Alan Pick started The Butcher Shop and Grill restaurant in Sandton, Johannesburg. He grew up around his parents' butchery in Kalk Bay and his travels around the world confirmed that customers are sick and tired of the overcooked, marinated, charred barbeque culture of steakhouses and wanted gourmet dinners. He is targeting customers with high disposable incomes, serves beef of a superior quality and is well known for his exclusive wines. An in-house butchery where customers can buy meat and biltong for home consumption and the integral Vintage Wine Cellar have also been added to the business.

- **From existing businesses:** There may be existing businesses in the same industry as you that leave gaps for you to take advantage of. For example, you want to convert your house into a restaurant, but don't know which market to capture. Think of your surrounding area and which customers you will find there. Say, for example, your house is close to a university, so you must cater for students, but it is also close to an office park, so you must also cater for corporate clients. You then think of a product that can be packaged to serve both these target groups – you can put picnic baskets together, basically two ranges, one for students and one for corporate clients. The basket contents and price must be different for each of the two main customer types.

- **From distributions channels:** Suppliers and wholesalers may also have ideas that can trigger a new product or service within your business. Talk to them as much as you can and find out what they need and what their problems are. You may be able to start a new business by solving one of their problems.

- **From the government Patent Office:** You can also go to the local Patent Office to find out which ideas already exist and where there are still gaps that must be filled.

- **From research and development:** Companies that focus on research and development may also be a valuable source to provide new ideas within your industry. Where do you think the idea of combining industries came from – for example, establishing a huge shopping mall combined with a theme park?

Let's share in some examples of creative ideas.

- The **Ice Mug** was created in response to a need that arose in California, in the USA. A law was brought in preventing people from taking bottles of cool drink or beer onto the beaches in California. Someone came up with the idea of making mugs out of ice and selling them at the beaches. People could then put their cool drink in the mug, and once they had finished drinking, they could just leave the mug on the sand to melt away.

- The **Baby Bath Tray** was created in response to the need mothers had when bathing their babies. It is very difficult to hold the baby and wash him/her at the same time. A tray was developed in which the baby lies safely inside the tub with his/her head above water, so that the mother's hands are free to wash her baby.

- **Soap leaves** is a product that was developed in response to the fact that we cannot always carry a bar of soap in our handbags with us, and therefore White Cottage Classics brought out a product that consists of ten 'leaves' of paper that have soap on them, so that you can wash your hands and throw the leaf away when you are finished.

2.7   ENTREPRENEURIAL OPPORTUNITIES

What is an opportunity and how does an entrepreneur exploit a feasible opportunity? An opportunity is defined by Hisrich and Peters (2002:39) as the process whereby the entrepreneur assesses whether a certain product, service or process has the necessary earnings potential based on the resource inputs that are required to manufacture and market it (for example, the entrepreneur makes a South African flag out of beads for R2,00 and sells it for R7,00). According to Nieman, Hough and Nieuwenhuizen (2003:54) the causal nature of opportunites needs to be assessed – thus, what leads to the existence of an opportunity? The following factors may result in an opportunity:

- **general and specific problems faced by consumers** (for example, ineffective public transport: Seela Moodley turned this problem into an opportunity by creating the Umhlanga Explorer, which offers airport, train-station and bus-station transfers, together with car and taxi services for companies and/or individual business executives);
- **technological changes** (for example, people can now buy their airline tickets over the Internet);
- **market shifts** (for example, SMS and e-mail communications are creating many opportunities to stay connected and in contact with your customers and offer them new services and products);
- **government regulations** (for example, the procurement policies of local governments create immense opportunities for previously disadvantaged entrepreneurs); and
- **competition** (for example, high levels of competition can create opportunities for new product development).

In a free enterprise system, opportunities are spawned when there are changing circumstances, chaos, confusion, inconsistencies, lags or leads, knowledge and information gaps, and a variety of other vacuums in an industry or market.

2.7.1   Ideas versus opportunities

At some point in your life, you may have had a brilliant idea, or so you thought. As you have probably realised by now, not all ideas are opportunities (i.e. they are not turned into a working business). How many people have thought of an idea but didn't take the leap and want to kick themselves later because it was developed into an opportunity by someone else?

An idea can become an opportunity when it is:

- **attractive:** it must be something that people want or need;
- **durable** (long lasting): will it still be a good idea six months from now?
- **timely:** the time when the entrepreneur enters the market is very important (it will normally be when competitors in the market have left gaps that you can take advantage of – this is called the window of opportunity); and

- **adds value:** an idea can only be an opportunity in the market when it can add value or substance to an existing product or service or alternatively to consumers' lives.

According to Timmons (2003:90), it is evident from the above that an idea is an opportunity when:
- the window of opportunity is open and will stay open long enough for an entrepreneur to enter the market;
- the management team can enter a market that is feasible and possesses the right characteristics;
- the venture is able to achieve a competitive advantage;
- the economics of venture are rewarding and forgiving and allow significant profit and growth potential;
- the opportunities are anchored in a product or service that adds value for its buyer or end user;
- the entrepreneur starts with what customers and the marketplace want and does not lose sight of this; and
- the entrepreneur has the perseverance to keep the venture running through difficult times.

2.7.2 Criteria to assess venture opportunities

The previous section discussed ideas as opposed to opportunities. It is also essential to know how to assess whether your opportunity is viable (workable) or not. You can use the following criteria to assess venture opportunities (Timmons, 2003:92).

- **Industry and market:** You should assess whether you have identified a market niche for a product or service that meets an important customer need and provides high value-added or value-created benefits to customers.
- **Economics:** The important aspect here is the break-even point (i.e. the point in time when you will sell enough products or services to cover your expenses) and whether a positive cash flow (i.e. a profit) is possible within two years. If the time to reach the break-even point and achieve a positive cash flow is greater that three years, the attractiveness of the opportunity decreases.
- **Exit issues:** Businesses that are eventually sold – privately or to the public – or acquired by someone else are usually started and grown with a harvest objective in mind (i.e. the owners want to leave the business with a profit). Planning is vital here, because, as it is often said, it is much harder to get out of a business than to get into it.
- **Competitive advantage issues:** Having a favourable window of opportunity is important. Having or being able to gain proprietary protection, regulatory advantage or other legal or contractual advantage, such as exclusive rights to a market or with a distributor, is attractive. Having or being able to gain an advantage in response/lead times is important, because these can create barriers to entry or expansion by others in the same market or business as you.

- **Management team:** A management track record of significant accomplishments in the industry, with the technology, and in the market area, with a proven profit and lots of achievement where the venture will compete is highly desirable.
- **Personal criteria:** You yourself, as the entrepreneur, will also determine whether the business will be successful or not. You must clearly define the goals of your venture and draw up a detailed, carefully thought out business plan that will serve as a roadmap to guide you. Your desire to succeed and your ability to cope with stress will also determine how your venture will be managed.
- **Strategic differentiation:** Do you have something in your business that is different from what your competitors offer? Does every aspect of your business work together like the links in a chain, so that if one link is not there it cannot operate? Some of these links in a business are the entrepreneurial team, the opportunity, the money and the people available in the business.

2.8 INTELLECTUAL PROPERTY: PROTECTING PRODUCTS/SERVICES

What do you do when you have evaluated your opportunity and gone through the assessment process and your opportunity has been turned into a great product or service? You have to protect that product or service.

In the tourism industry, you will find that registering your **trademark** is the best way to protect your business. A trademark can be words, names, symbols or other devices that distinguish your goods or services. A trademark is protected for ten years and must be renewed after that period for a further ten years. The trademark protects your right to stop others from using similar trademarks that might cause confusion or deception regarding the protected item (Lumsdaine & Binks, 2003:138).

For example, those delightful and delicious peppers that so tantalise our tastebuds are called **Piquanté Peppers** and, whether whole or as a sauce, are **only available under the PEPPADEW™ brand**. This is because PEPPADEW INTERNATIONAL has international growing rights for Piquanté Peppers and nobody else can grow them.

The company is trying to create media and consumer awareness of the fact that only PEPPADEW INTERNATIONAL grows and bottles Piquanté Peppers under the PEPPADEW™ brand.

PEPPADEW™ Piquanté Peppers are the first new fruit discovery since the Kiwi fruit (and that was 26 years ago!). They are delicious, they are unique, and they were developed right here in South Africa!

Another way of protecting a product is by registering a **patent**. A patent gives the exclusive right to an inventor to make, use or sell his/her invention. There are two types of patents.

- **Design patent:** Here the patent protects only the appearance of an article, but not its structural or functional features. The Weber Braai is an example of a product that has a design patent, which means nobody can copy its exact features and appearance.
- **Utility patent:** This covers the function of a product; in other words, how it operates. The Pastel Accounting software program is an example of a utility patent, where nobody can copy the way in which the program works.

A patent can offer 20 years of protection on the specific product or service.

2.9 HOW TO ESTABLISH A SUSTAINABLE COMPETITIVE ADVANTAGE

Every entrepreneur should have a competitive edge; so what is yours? A competitive edge or competitive advantage is something that an entrepreneur's product or service has that makes it better and more attractive than the product/service of his or her competitors in the same industry. It is even better when you have a *sustainable* competitive advantage, i.e. when you have such an edge over your competitors that your product/service cannot be copied or followed by competitors, with the result that your competitive advantage will last a long time.

The Hotelbon in The Netherlands is a good example of a sustainable competitive advantage in the tourism industry. The Hotelbon is a booklet that contains discount vouchers that travellers and tourists can use to pay for hotels, car rental, restaurants, etc. in Europe. It is the only product of its kind and is used by thousands of tourists every month. Competitors that try to copy this concept are going to struggle due to the image Hotelbon has established in the market. Tourists know that the products and services that they find in the Hotelbon booklet are of high quality and provide good value for money.

2.9.1 How to create a competitive advantage

According to Nieman, Niewenhuizen and Hough (2003:85), the following factors can guide you on how you can establish a competitive advantage.

- **Price/Value:** Price is a not a sustainable competitive advantage. It only has a short-term advantage because it can only be a competitive advantage when your price is lower than your competitors' prices. They can also lower their prices, so it is easy to copy.
- **Customer convenience:** It is said that if you can make life more convenient for your customers, only then will you have loyal customers. An example would be if you have a bed-and-breakfast guesthouse and you offer to fetch visitors from the airport when they arrive, as part of their visit.
- **Customer experience:** If you can leave your business's imprint in the minds of your customers and make them remember you, you will have an edge over the rest. For example,

McDonald's focuses on children and wants them to remember their visits by giving them free toys with their meals.

- **Notable product attributes:** Any products that have specific attributes that make them known in the market will establish a competitive advantage, such as cell phones with special features.
- **Unique service features:** Customer service is a must for any business and must be the essence of every business. The staff of Prada, an international clothing store, are trained to remember every customer's name and fashion style and will aim to please that customer when he/she comes into the store. They are even trained to remember how each customer likes his/her coffee or tea.

EXERCISES

2.10 PRACTICAL EXERCISES: HOW TO GET THOSE CREATIVE JUICES FLOWING

Here is a practical exercise for you to try: Take a paperclip and think of as many unordinary uses for it as you can in five minutes. Write them down and choose those that are unique and new.

P.S. If you came up with more than ten new, unique ideas, your creative juices are really flowing.

Another exercise: Link the nine dots below **by using only four straight lines and without lifting your pen from the paper**.

2.11 SUMMARY

You should now know what elements you need in order to be creative and how to be more creative. It is important to make sure that you have a good opportunity and that the opportunity will be received well in the market and satisfy some or other need. Your creativity should provide you with that opportunity. Creative problem-solving is essential for any entrepreneur; but it is important to remember that there are certain blocks to creativity that can prevent you from being creative. By being aware of them, you should be able to overcome them.

2.12 IMPORTANT WEBSITES TO EXPLORE

- The website Creativity at Work is a rich resource for developing personal creativity and organisational innovation in the workplace. Explore the thinking and perceiving skills of artists, scientists, inventors, leaders and visionaries through the articles on this site.

  www.creativityatwork.com/

- On the Innovation Creativity & Entrepreneurship Zone (ICE) website you can read about the bright ideas, business plans and success stories that other ICE Zone members have come up with. Be sure to check out the Classified Ads section to seek out new business ventures or sell your products.

  www.northeast.org.sg/icezone/home_content.jsp

- Thinking 'outside the box' is essential if you wish to succeed as an entrepreneur. Innovative thinking, brainstorming and creativity exercises are encouraged and used by forward-thinking businesses and corporations to successfully plan, create, and sell products and services. This portal will lead you to some very interesting websites about creativity:

  www.creativity-portal.com

3 Starting Your Own Business

Melodi Botha

Once you have worked through this chapter, you should be able to:

☞ Know how to start your own business

☞ Understand the reasons why people start their own businesses

☞ Be aware of the influences on the start-up decision

☞ Know what is required to start a business

☞ Be aware of the ten simple rules for a successful start-up

☞ Identify an ideal location for your business

3.1 INTRODUCTION

Do you dream about becoming a tour operator, a travel agent or maybe a hotel manager? All of these careers have some element in them of working for yourself. Entrepreneurship is the buzzword that hangs on everybody's lips when talking about starting your own business. Existing entrepreneurs will tell you that starting your own business is very self-satisfying, but at the same time extremely hard work.

Entrepreneurship – or being an entrepreneur – is not always for every person, as you must be able to create something out of nothing and add value to a product or service in some or other way, which not everyone is able to do.

Before we go any further, it is important to learn how other entrepreneurs started their businesses. Take note of the following examples that will explain entrepreneurship a bit further.

Ntandi Fatji is very good with beadwork, so she decided to turn her passion into a business and started making beaded products such as South African flags, jewellery and mugs from her house and selling them at taxi ranks. Her products became so popular that she opened her own shop in a shopping centre across the street from the busiest taxi rank. She currently employees 59 people and her business just keeps growing and growing.

Let's use the business called Chip-away to illustrate entrepreneurship and small business management.

Chip-away is a new, innovative business that was established and is managed by the Potato sisters. They saw the need for tasty, affordable fast food at sports and other entertainment events. The Potato sisters realised that many customers cannot afford or do not like the other snacks available on the market. Biltong, for instance, is not very filling; and there is also an insufficient variety of snacks available. Endless time standing in queues, waiting to be served, frustrates spectators, because of the amount of time taken for food preparation.

Each Chip-away employee wears exactly the same uniform, and there is one person responsible for working with the money. Chip-away carts are built according to the same specifications. Each cart is equipped with a fryer, and carries a variety of sauces. The Potato sisters operated the first Chip-away themselves, and thereafter opened a franchise of Chip-away carts. (They are thus the franchisors of Chip-away.) As competitors have entered the market, the trend of similar fast food services has become more widespread. The early innovative stage has passed, but the entrepreneurs who started the enterprise (the Potato sisters) are constantly seeking new ideas to help Chip-away work better and to encourage growth of the business.

The first addition to Chip-away was the trailer-type shop carrying refreshments and plain and very basic fries. It was successfully implemented and is constantly being refined by means of improved sauces, product variety and built-in controls. One of the next projected expansions is to franchise, and this will soon be undertaken by the owners.

The entrepreneurs who started Chip-away are clearly innovative and creative, and have intentions of development and growth. We can say that the founders and owners of Chip-away are entrepreneurs, small business managers and franchisors.

The franchisees are the people who then go out and buy a Chip-away from the entrepreneurs who started Chip-away. These small business managers both manage and run the Chip-away themselves or employ staff to operate it. When the sites for a Chip-away have been identified and approved by the franchisors, the unit will be erected by them and fitted to their own specifications. Chip-away franchisees must manage their enterprises according to strict directives drawn up by the franchisors that they (the franchisors) consider to be essential for success.

3.2 REASONS FOR THE START-UP PHENOMENON

There are various reasons why people start businesses and we need to explore them.

It has become evident that entrepreneurship is not necessarily seen as something people want to do. Many South Africans are forced into the path of entrepreneurship because of retrenchment, job frustration or job losses. This section of the chapter focuses on the main reasons that drive individuals to become entrepreneurs. These reasons can be classified as either opportunity (**pull factors**) or necessity (**push factors**) (Nieman, Hough and Nieuwenhuizen, 2003:31).

Push factors are those factors that force people to become entrepreneurs; for example, because traditional jobs are less attractive, or because an individual does not have any other career choice or option. They include:

- unemployment, i.e. when a person does not have a job in the established economy;
- job insecurity; for example, if a person is only appointed on a contract basis for a short period;
- disagreement with management, career limitations and setbacks in a conventional job;
- if someone does not 'fit in' to an organisation;
- the inability to develop a personal innovation in a conventional job;
- the limitations of financial rewards from conventional jobs; and
- if someone has no other alternative.

Pull factors are those factors that encourage people in traditional jobs to leave those jobs in order to become entrepreneurs. They include the attractions of:

- independence – the freedom to work for oneself;
- the sense of achievement gained from successfully running one's own venture;
- recognition – the desire to gain the social standing achieved by successfull entrepreneurs;
- personal development – the freedom to pursue personal innovation; and
- personal wealth – the financial rewards of entrepreneurship.

The number of entrepreneurs operating at any one time will depend on the strength of the push and pull forces. If they are strong, then a large number of entrepreneurs will emerge.

Most people face a combination of both push and pull factors, as illustrated in Figure 3.1 and in the example below.

Patricia Stafford is a 55-year-old mother of four, and all of her children have moved out of their huge house to live on their own. She worked for a large organisation for 20 years and got retrenched. She has been thinking about starting her own bed-and-breakfast guesthouse for a long time and thought that this is the ideal opportunity to do so. She did her market

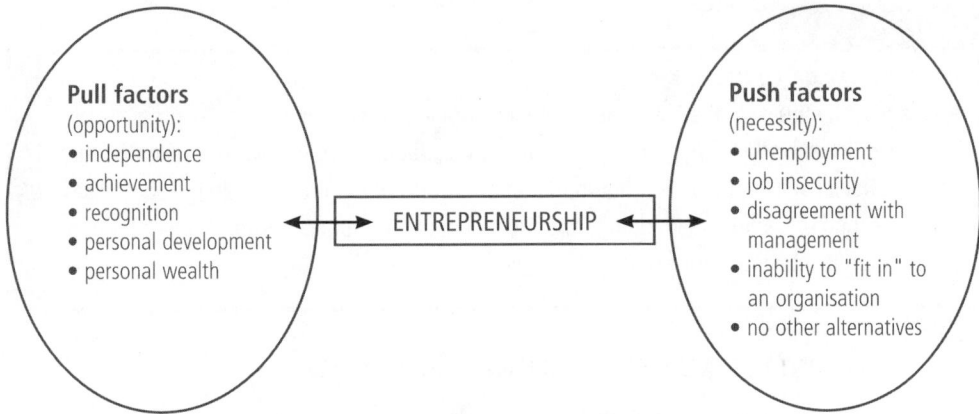

Figure 3.1: The push and pull factors of entrepreneurship

Source: Adapted from Nieman, Hough and Niewenhuizen (2003:31)

research and found that a need existed for a B & B in her area. Therefore she opened the B & B because she didn't have a job any more (necessity) and because the need existed for a B & B in the area (opportunity).

3.3   INFLUENCES ON THE START-UP DECISION

Various factors can be seen to influence the decision of an entrepreneur to start his or her own business:

- the previous influences on the entrepreneur; e.g. his/her background, family, age, education, work experience, etc.;
- the organisation in which he/she had previously been working; e.g. its location, market sector, skills required, etc.; and
- the environmental factors external to the individual that contribute to the decision; e.g. the state of the economy, role models, advice, staff, etc.

Two people looked out from prison bars.
One saw the mud, the other saw stars.

Author unknown

> **Kwa Mothakga Lodge in Klerksdorp**
> Diakanyo Khunou's mother and father owned a guesthouse when she was growing up. Because of her background, she also started a guesthouse – the Kwa Mothakga Lodge, which prides itself on providing accommodation at affordable rates. The lodge specialises in the hosting of traditional weddings and the making of traditional cuisine. It has 22 rooms and conference facilities for up to 100 people.

3.4   SO YOU WANT TO START YOUR OWN BUSINESS! NOW WHAT?

Why do some businesses fail while others succeed? Is there a magic formula that must be followed to ensure that a new start-up business survives and succeeds? Different things work for different entrepreneurs, but there are some basic requirements that you need to start a business. These requirements are as follows.

- **You have to have a workable idea of something that can make money**

TIP: It must be something that other people WANT/NEED. For example, Maria lived on a farm with the most wonderful juicy lemons and she decided to make her own lemonade and sell it to the people that live and work on surrounding farms.

> When fate hands us a lemon, let's try to make lemonade.
>
> *Julius Rosenwald*

- **Gather as much information and knowledge as possible** (chapter 6 of this book deals with this much more extensively)

TIP: Get help from entrepreneurs, role models and those already running their own businesses. Maria asked her uncle for advice because he operates his own hardware store in town and he could assist her with problems like where to begin and how to sell her lemonade.

- **You must have customers.**

TIP: It's easier to sell the product or service to people who want or need it, and those people are your customers. Maria sold the lemonade to thirsty people in the surrounding area.

- **You must know your competitors**

TIP: You must always be aware that there are others doing the same thing; they are called your, *competitors*. BE AWARE OF THEM!!! Always try to have better products/services than them. There might be shops in Maria's surrounding area that are already selling lemonade and other fruit juices.

- **You must have a marketing strategy**

TIP: If you have a great business, but nobody knows about it, customers will not come to you – you have to advertise and do marketing. Maria went to all the surrounding farms and gave out samples of her lemonade so that her customers could taste it. Now she comes by every morning at 7 o'clock to take orders for the day.

- **In the end, it will all depend on you and whether you have the passion and dedication to see your idea for a new business through.**

TIP: Remember it's not all glamour – it takes hard work and still more hard work to make it on your own. Maria works very hard, and she's up at 4 o'clock every morning to prepare her lemonade for the day's orders. Remember: It's not the hours you put in – it's what you put in those hours!!!

3.5   TEN SIMPLE RULES FOR A SUCCESSFUL START-UP

Rule 1: Choose a business that's right for you

The key here is to choose an option that will fit into your lifestyle and not just do something because everybody else is doing it; for example, if your passion is dancing, it would probably be a good idea to open a dance studio in your neighbourhood. **Work with what you know and are good at.**

Rule 2: Do your market research

Make sure you find out whether kids in the area want to learn how to dance and would support your dance studio. Find out what it will cost. What will you have to buy or get to start the business; for example, open floor space, a CD player and CDs, should you rent or buy the studio, etc.?

Rule 3: Draw up a business plan

A business plan is a written document that you must draw up that puts all your plans on paper. Refer to chapter 4 to see how to prepare a business plan. Successful businesses are properly planned businesses.

Rule 4: Choose a specialist investor

An investor is someone who gives you money to help you start or grow your business and wants to share in the profits. Family member are often the easiest 'source' from which you can obtain money to start you business. Choose someone that will support you and will trust you with their money, if you don't have money of your own. Refer to chapter 6 to see how you should choose an investor.

Rule 5: Choose the right people to work for you

Remember that when you have your own business, you are the boss and people will work for you. Make sure you have capable, loyal and honest people working for you. It can destroy a business if employees are unethical or do not get along with their boss or one another.

Rule 6: Market your business

You have to make people aware of the products or services that you are providing in your business. There are different ways to communicate information about your business to your customers. You can use radio, newspapers, bulletin boards in the area, pamphlets or word-of-mouth (i.e. when customers talk about your business). They say that WORD-OF-MOUTH is the most effective source of marketing. Remember: When people are satisfied with your business, they will tell five other people; when they are dissatisfied, they will tell ten other people!!! Therefore word-of-mouth is only effective if it is positive!

Rule 7: Put in financial systems from the start

Make sure you keep accurate records of all the money you use, as well as the money that comes into your business. Many businesses fail because they do not have systems to keep accurate track of how much money they spend and how much they make.

Rule 8: Manage your cash flow

Cash flow is cash that comes into the business and cash that goes out of the business. It is the physical money that you have in you handbag or pocket! Remember that if you don't have cash available to pay your bills, your business will fail.

Cash flow is the life blood of your business. Plan it. Know it. Live by it every day!

Rule 9: Supplement your own knowledge with specialist skills

If you do not know all there is to know about your business, make sure you employ people that can fill that gap and assist you where you don't have strong points. Luckily, people differ and everybody is good at different things. You and your employees should complement one another in your business.

Rule 10: Enjoy yourself

This is the most important rule of all. If you're not enjoying yourself while you're running your own business, there isn't much point in doing it.

3.6 LOCATION OF THE BUSINESS

The location of a business is extremely important – it can be the main reason why your business succeeds or fails. Especially in the tourism industry, one often wonders why a hotel in a certain area is more successful than an almost identical hotel in another area. The difference obviously lies in their locations! It is very important to remember that choosing a location for your business is permanent and you are in it for the long run! According to Nieman, Hough and Niewenhuizen (2003:137), you should be able to determine the specific success factors impacting on your chosen business in the location you choose. Some general factors related to your business's location you should consider are:

- target market (who your customers are going to be);
- availability of raw material and suppliers;
- support and technical infrastructure;
- transport infrastructure;
- availability of labour and skills;
- climate conditions;
- seasonality; and
- political and social stability.

Location can be subdivided into three general functional categories.

- **Site**

This includes availability of land, basic utilities, amenities (quality of life), and the nature and level of access to local transportation. These factors have an important effect on the costs associated with a location. For example, the Rose and Crown Guest Lodge is situated in the city of Nelspruit, Mpumalanga and guests will happily pay not only for the accommodation, but also for the breathtaking view of the imposing mountains and a wonderful view of the city of Nelspruit.

- **Accessibility**

This includes a number of opportunity factors related to a location, mainly labour (wages, availability, level of qualification), materials (availability, cost), energy, markets (local, regional and global), and accessibility to suppliers and customers.

- **Infrastructure**

Is it important that your location be convenient to transportation or to suppliers? Do you need your customers to have easy walk-in access to your business? What are your requirements for parking, and proximity to motorways, airports, and rail and shipping centres? Construction? Most new companies should not sink capital into construction, but if you are planning to build, then costs and specifications will be a major part of your plan.

- Cost: Estimate your occupation expenses, including rent, but also including maintenance, utilities, insurance and initial remodelling costs to make the premises suit your needs. These amounts will become part of your financial plan.
- What will be your business hours (when will you be open for business)?

The Zwinoni Lodge is situated in Milnerton Ridge with spectacular views of the Rietvlei Nature Reserve. It has seven rooms in the main house and two additional rooms in the cottage. The house is decorated to reflect the different cultures of South African hospitality.

3.7 THE PRODUCT LIFE CYCLE

The product life cycle is another important aspect that you as entrepreneur have to be aware of when starting a business. This consists of the stages each product or service goes through from introduction to decline.

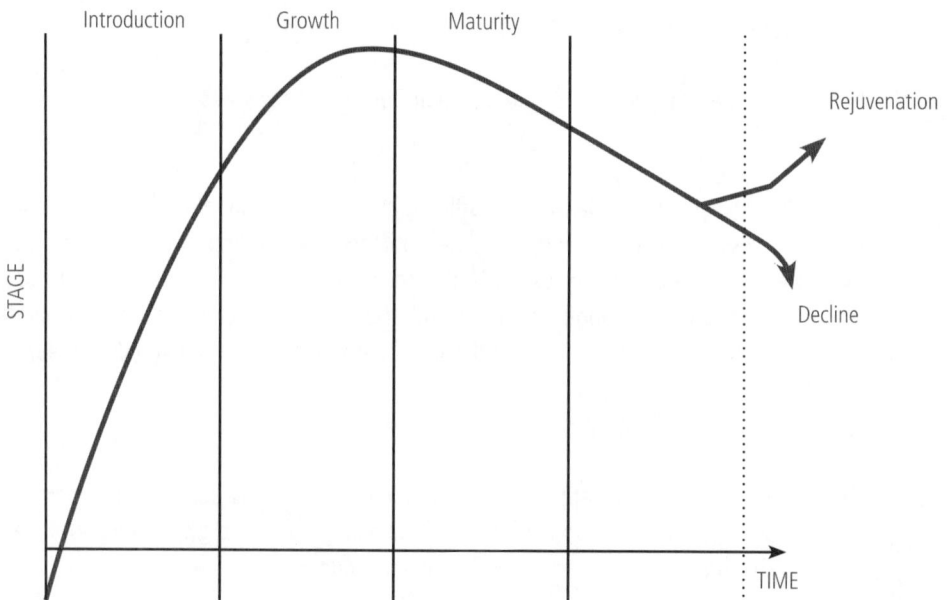

Figure 3.2: **Product life cycle**

Stage 1: Introduction

During this first stage, the product gets introduced to the market. You need to spend a lot of effort on marketing and promoting your business.

Stage 2: Growth

During this stage, the product is known in the market and ideally grows to such an extent that the business really takes off.

Stage 3: Maturity

The product has now reached maturity; in other words, it has now stabilised in the market, and creativity and innovation might be needed to keep it popular.

Stage 4: Decline/Rejuvenation

During this stage, the demand for the product has started to decline. As the entrepreneur, you have two choices: to let the product die or rejuvenate it by improving the marketing or introducing innovations that make it attractive to its customers once more.

Case study: Talking Beads, a company owned by Tembeka Nkamba van Wyk

Talking Beads was launched in May 1997. When growing up as a young girl in the Eastern Cape, Nkamba van Wyk was very aware of the disparities surrounding her, not only in terms of poverty, but also in terms of race, gender and religion. She thought that adults would be concerned about these things, but grew to realise that they were not bold enough to face them and address them, and that young people were more liberated in expressing such concerns.

Later, working in the corporate environment, she saw corporate gifts being bought from Taiwan and the United States; always things like cufflinks, pens and silk ties. When tasked one year to buy the gifts, she persuaded her boss to let her buy local rural crafts instead. Some time later, working in communications in government, she spoke to Mama Tswana, a street vendor selling vetkoek, who complained that business was very bad. In their discussion, it came out that Mama Tswana knew how to do beadwork. That was the start of an ongoing initiative. After much badgering of possible customers to accept this kind of thing, and much persuading of people that these gifts could be produced on time and in quantity, and that they would be well received, the business got under way.

Nkamba van Wyk eventually gave up a 'cushy' job to concentrate on Talking Beads. Everybody discouraged her, but she stood her ground. Keys to her success have been collaboration and taking on new challenges.

Some of the hard-earned lessons she has learned are as follows.

- Pricing is a problem, especially for rural women, but it is better to walk away from an order, poor and proud, than accept it at a price that won't even cover the costs.
- Another pitfall to be wary of is trade missions, where there is sometimes a lack of quality control and your quality products get lumped together with inferior ones. Ideally, there should be a preliminary exhibition prior to the trade mission, to establish quality levels and

even possibly have someone from the relevant country giving opinions on the type of goods that might work in their country.

- It is very important to establish international links, especially if you are exporting your goods.

- It is also necessary to have suitable outlets – not flea markets, but a central place where traders from all over the world can be invited to come and place orders; for example, a trade centre for top-of-the-range crafts, including items such as cutlery, table top items, linen and beautiful furniture.

- Databanks are needed in the different sectors so that people can collaborate and find the right partners.

- You also need to look very carefully at the system of payment, especially to small businesses who cannot get credit and do not have good cash flow. Ideally, there should be a 50% deposit when placing the order, with the balance payable on delivery. This will help small businesses to survive.

To sum up her experience and philosophy of life, Nkamba van Wyk wrote the following poem.

I'm a South African
by Tembeka Nkamba van Wyk

I am a country girl
I'm born of great kings and queens of this continent.

I am a descendant of the mighty
who survived droughts, floods, diseases, famine,
even prosecution by apartheid laws and others.

My heritage has survived.
My heritage survived, being cast away by religious fanatics
who believed beads were bad while pearls were pretty.

Brewing our own beer was evil, backward and sinful,
while buying Castle and Lion was decent and sophisticated.

I am the princess of beads,
I am the mother of intricate creations.

With my teeny long fingers I just weave together,
bead by bead, the small colourful grains from abroad
and make a statement.

I just dream of a day
when all South Africans will have a home
and a daily ration,
when every child will go to school
and every sick person will afford medication,
when crime will be a folktale from the past,
when this, our land, will be a paradise,
adored and nurtured by visitors from far and wide;
a place for pilgrimage for all, from the world over.

Then we will have arrived.

3.8   CONCLUSION

In this chapter, a number of key issues and step were discussed. To sum up: starting a business demands that you have in place the following key elements in order to ensure that your business will grow:

- a great entrepreneurial opportunity;
- the passion to start and drive your business;
- relevant, comprehensive information about your business and sound market research;
- customers that will support you;
- proper marketing for your business;
- the right location for your business;
- the right infrastructure to run your business; and
- a sound management team and capable, enthusiastic employees.

3.9   IMPORTANT NUMBERS TO KEEP AND WEBSITES TO EXPLORE

- Business Referral and Information Network (BRAIN) provides advice and information for young entrepreneurs on all aspects of starting a business. They can be visited at www.brain.org.za

Postal address:
BRAIN National SMME Information Centre
7th Floor, 1 Dr Lategan Road Groenkloof Pretoria 0181
P O Box 395 Pretoria 0001
E-mail: There is an e-mail enquiry form on the website or: offersn@namac.co.za
Tel: 0860-103-703

- Companies and Intellectual Property Registration Office (CIPRO) can help you to register your business and assist you with the registration of trademarks and patents.
  Postal address:
  P O Box 429 Pretoria 0001
  Physical address:
  The DTI campus (Block F)
  77 Meintjies Street Sunnyside Pretoria
  Customer contact centre:
  Tel: 0861-843-384
  Fax: 0861-843-888
  Website: www.cipro.gov.za/home
- Business Partners is a specialist investment company that provides debt and equity investments to small businesses.
  Area offices:

JOHANNESBURG
Business Partners Centre
3 Caxton Road Industria Johannesburg
P O Box 4300 Johannesburg 2000
Tel: 011-470-3111
Fax: 011-470-3123

DURBAN
Business Partners Centre
23 Jan Hofmeyr Road Westville
P O Box 636 Westville 3630
Tel: 031-240-7700
Fax: 031-266-7286

CAPE TOWN
Business Partners Centre
60 Sir Lowry Road Cape Town
P O Box 4295 Cape Town 8000
Tel: 021-464-3600
Fax: 021-461-8720

PORT ELIZABETH
266 Govan Mbeki Avenue Port Elizabeth
P O Box 1745 Port Elizabeth 6000
Tel: 041-582-1601
Fax: 041-585-2297
Website: www.businesspartners.co.za

- Umsobomvu Youth Fund is a catalyst organisation facilitating the creation of opportunities for youth employment and youth entrepreneurship by making investments that deliver effective programmes. Umsobomvu conceptualises and designs programmes and contracts suitable service providers for implementing them.
Tel: 011-805-9701
Fax: 011-805-9709
Postal address: P O Box 982 Halfway House 1685
Physical address: Block P, Cental Park 16th Road Midrand
E-mail: info@uyf.org.za
Website: www.umsobomvu.org.za

- Real Business Network is a membership club that hosts networking sessions where you will be able to explore business opportunities with other entrepreneurs.
Contact details:
For Network issues and events: Jayne Boccaleone
Real Business Network Manager
E-mail: manager@realbusiness.co.za
Tel: 044-381-0107
For editorial issues: Colin Anthony,
Editor, Real Business
E-mail: editor@realbusiness.co.za
Tel: 011-280-5558
Website: www.realbusiness.co.za

- Buzzline, the South African student portal, can assist you with running a small business and how to make money. It also specialises in student investments.
Website: www.buzzline.co.za

- Swiss-South African Co-operation Initiative Funding Programme (SSACI Funding Programme) SSACI's overall objective in terms of its deed of trust is: 'To advance educational opportunities for disadvantaged young South Africans in order to enable them to obtain employment.' This is in line with one of the South African government's own priorities, namely to tackle the critical problem of youth unemployment.
Contact details:
Postal address:
Private Bag X37 Hatfield 0028
Physical address:
Unit 4, Parkfield Court 1185 Park Street Hatfield Pretoria
E-mail: ssaci@sdc.net
 Tel: 012-362-2972
Fax: 012-362-2971
Website: www.ssaci.org.za

4 The Business Plan

Melodi Botha

Once you have worked through this chapter, you should be able to:

☞ Understand why it is necessary to prepare a business plan
☞ Prepare a feasibility study for your business
☞ Be aware of the elements that should be included in a business plan
☞ Prepare a business plan for your business
☞ Present a business plan to peers
☞ Know why some business plans fail

4.1 INTRODUCTION

Entrepreneurs worldwide will agree that prospective entrepreneurs need a business plan when starting their own businesses, because it is seen as a roadmap for the future of that business. A business plan is merely a complete action plan or forecast of how you plan or intend to achieve your business goals. It is a public document and is important to the entrepreneur him-/herself, investors, bankers and employees. It is vitally important for you to do your planning before starting your business – many entrepreneurs fail because they did not do so. It is also essential for you to write your own business plan or be involved when writing the business plan for your business – don't leave it to someone else who doesn't have the in-depth understanding of your business that you have. This chapter will highlight why a business plan and planning is important and how you should draw up a business plan. Furthermore, it will illustrate all the essential elements that you must include when writing your business plan. The last section of the chapter will also highlight the most important reasons why business plans are not successful in obtaining funding.

It usually takes several weeks to complete a good business plan, and most of that time is spent in research and re-thinking your ideas and assumptions in order to create the best plan possible. But that is the value of the process, so make time to do the job properly – those who do take the time never regret the effort. And finally, be sure to keep detailed notes on your sources of information and the assumptions underlying your financial data.

4.2 WHY IS PLANNING NEEDED?

> If you don't know where you're going, you probably won't get there.
>
> Forrest Gump

Planning is the process that can help to determine where you are going, how you are going to get there and also how you will know when you've arrived at your destination. Your business plan can be seen as a roadmap that will make sure you reach your destination. If you start a business without a business plan, you may still be successful, but you might take longer to get there (and remember that there is also a good chance that your business will fail if you don't plan properly). You will almost certainly make more mistakes than you would have if you had done the proper planning and market research and prepared a proper business plan before you started your business.

> It takes time to succeed, because success is merely the natural reward of taking time to do anything well!
>
> Joseph Ross

4.3 REASONS FOR DRAWING UP A BUSINESS PLAN

There are several reasons why you should draw up a business plan, but the most important reasons are as follows.

- **For your own use**
  It is important to have all your ideas written down on paper and then your business plan will assist you in turning those ideas into reality. Firstly, it makes you think through your ideas more carefully. Secondly, it ensures that you don't forget any of your ideas. And thirdly, it helps you to take a second look at your ideas to make sure that they will actually work. It is also a roadmap to keep you on track when you are running your own business.

- **To obtain funding**
  Another important reason is to obtain money to start or grow your business. All financial institutions, investors, business angels, business partners and other financial organisations insist on receiving a business plan from entrepreneurs when the entrepreneurs apply for finance.

> Starting a business requires 10% capital and 90% guts.
>
> Raymond Ackerman

- **To help others understand your business**
  A business plan is a public document and should be given to employees, suppliers and other stakeholders to read when dealing with your business. Only then will they understand your business completely and know how to help it succeed.

- **As a tool to reduce risk**
  Because a business plan can be used as a roadmap, it helps to reduce the risk of losing money, in the same way that a real roadmap helps prevent you from getting lost. It can also reduce the risk of failure. Remember that running a business is not merely rolling a dice and hoping for a six; it is careful planning to make *sure* you throw a six!

4.4 THE FEASIBILITY STUDY

Before committing time and energy to preparing a business plan, you should do a quick feasibility study of the idea you have for a business. A feasibility study assesses whether your business plan is realistic and whether it is likely to work; in other words, it checks whether your idea for a business is a viable and workable business opportunity. You must do the feasibility study before you prepare to write your business plan. (There is no point in spending time writing a business plan for a business idea that is not feasible.) There are ten easy steps that you should follow in order to prepare a feasibility study.

Step 1: List all elements of the business plan

The table of contents of the actual business plan must be listed in the first step of the feasibility study. This is seen as a checklist to ensure that you do not repeat things when you are drawing up the actual business plan.

Step 2: Include a summary/overview of your business

This section must be the 'attention-getter' – it must be exciting and interesting! What makes your business different/unique? It is necessary to define the market you will operate in and list the products/services you will deliver. In chapter 2, the sustainable competitive advantage was discussed; you must refer back to that section when preparing this step of the feasibility study. Your business must have a sustainable competitive advantage if it is to succeed.

Step 3: List your goals and objectives

Business objectives are about facts – not fiction! List what you as the entrepreneur want to achieve within the next six to 12 months. The objectives must be clear and *achievable/attainable*; in other words, they must be things that you can actually achieve within that time period. It is important to take one objective at a time and not try and do everything at once.

Step 4: Define your business

Are you starting a PRODUCT- or SERVICE-based business? Often your business will be a combination of these; for example, think about visiting a travel agency. The products that you will receive are the airline ticket and hotel accommodation, but the customer service that you receive while making the booking with the travel agent is seen as the service element. Service in the tourism industry refers to the service that the customer receives from the employee that deals with that customer.

Factors that you need to consider:

- **Supply source:** Who will be your suppliers, if any? Do you have 'back-up' suppliers (in other words, if your suppliers are not available, who else can you use)?
- **The range of products and services that you can offer to your customers**
- **Presentation and packaging:** Consider not only the physical packaging that is around a product, but also the presentation of the people in your business that deal with customers. For example, all staff at the Southern Sun Hotel Group wear the same uniform to create unity within the business.
- **How will you present yourself and your business?** Let's use the following Avis story as an example. When I rented a car from Avis at Durban International Airport, there was an ice cold cool drink in the car when it was delivered to me. It was a very hot and humid day in Durban, and I thought somebody else had forgotten their cool drink in the car, so I went back to the Avis lady to give it to her. But she explained that since it was a very hot day, the driver of every car that went out that day would receive a cool drink! That really made my day, and I've been a loyal user of Avis Car Rental ever since!
- **Know you distribution channels:** How will your products/services get from where they are made/produced to where they are sold?
- **Building after-sales relationships:** This is one of the most important things to remember when starting a new business. You have to keep a database of your customers to make sure you follow up on any business you do with them and to keep reminding them about your business by sending them valuable information. For example, when you have special deals such as cruises or tours at very affordable prices, it is a good idea to let your loyal customers know about them.
- **Patent and protect your ideas:** If you have a secret that is worth keeping, make sure you patent it at the patent office, stationed regionally in South Africa.
- **Build brand identity:** Holiday Inn Hotels are well known throughout the world because the company works hard at building a brand for itself. You must do the same for your business.

Step 5: Define your target market

Make sure you have considered the following.

- **Is there a market for your product?** Is there really a need for that specific product or service?
- **Narrow down your target market** – it is virtually impossible to reach all the people in the world, so decide who your main customers are and focus on them.

- **Choose a market that has potential for growth** – for example, people will always need food, that is why restaurants that sell good food and give value for money are so successful.
- **Keep abreast of market trends** – for example, trends such as the explosion of coffee shops and B & Bs during the last three years and how this can be combined with art galleries, book shops and even hair-dressing salons.
- **Select the right geographic site** – i.e. close to your target market.
- **Think of seasonal strategies:** This is something that is particularly relevant to the tourism industry and should be taken into account when starting your business.
- **Beware of competition:** Make sure that you know your competitors and the products and services that they provide and how they differ from your products and services.

Step 6: Get your business's infrastructure right: The building blocks of success

The infrastructure that surrounds you when starting your own business consists of the following important aspects.

- **Location, Location, LOCATION!!** This can make or break your business – consumers nowadays want absolute convenience, and the moment they find it difficult to get access to your product/service, they won't bother trying.
- **Staff** – invest in high quality staff.
- **Training and development** must take place continuously. Set high standards from the start and make sure that there are training possibilities for staff and management in order to uplift their skills.
- **Systems and controls** – technology. Be there as it happens, and don't let someone else make your decisions in this area for you! Make your life easier by having the appropriate systems in place when starting your business.
- **Operations manuals** – 'paint by numbers' for success. Make sure that you have a three-to-four-page document that is given to every new staff member or partner that joins your business. It will include your rules and regulations on things such as lunch hour, dress code, office/working hours, etc.

Step 7: Prepare a SWOT-analysis

Determine your definite and possible **S**trengths, **W**eaknesses, **O**pportunities and **T**hreats (**SWOT**). Give an honest assessment of the risks you face in relation to the potential for growth, profitability and capital appreciation. It is important not only to specify your strengths, but also to indicate how you will capitalise on those strengths. It is also vital to indicate how you are going to address (overcome) your weaknesses.

Here is an example of a SWOT-analysis done for a company called Instead of Flowers … Box It! The company provides exactly what the name says: customised gift boxes instead of flowers. PLEASE NOTE: It is important not only to mention the strengths, weaknesses, opportunities and threats of you business, but also to indicate what you are going to do *about them*, as illustrated below.

Strengths (inside the business)	Capitalise on strengths
1. Alliance with high quality suppliers	1. Market entry and gaining market knowledge
2. Quality and fresh products with unique features	2. Favourable consumer perception
3. Successfully test marketed in South Africa	3. After-sale care is provided to test customer satisfaction, recommendations and comments
4. Skilled and committed team	4. Management has skills and experience in a variety of areas
5. High margins on gift box content	5. Ability to negotiate on bulk purchases
6. Low set-up costs	6. This reduces capital costs and the business is an extension of the main business, which has all the operational systems and controls in place
7. Continuous training is provided	
8. Good location	7. This enhances product features and improves skills and creative ways of thinking
9. Penetrate corporate market	8. Central and close to suppliers and main customers
	9. Expand corporate market by keeping current clients and gaining new clients through intensive marketing
Weaknesses (inside the business)	**Address weaknesses**
1. Reliance on a few clients initially	1. Committed to expansion
2. Management team has not worked together for long	2. High margins provide flexibility
3. Sales team not yet in place	3. Professional sales team recruited with assistance of venture partners who will have affinity with and experience in the food/ beverage and other produce industries
4. Staff has limited international experience	
5. Cash-flow problems	4. Addressed by introductions through management to conduct market research on countries that are considered for exporting
6. Limited financing	
7. Shortage of personnel	
8. Networking	5. Manage cash flow in terms of following up on debtors and their payment terms
9. Communication barrier with small, remote supplier	6. Prepare a business plan that will enable the company to apply for finance and expand the business's horizons
	7. As the company grows, new personnel with the right expertise will be hired
	8. Provide after-sales care to clients to ensure that current clients are kept
	9. Through a growing mobile network, this is slowly disappearing

Opportunities (outside the business)	Maximise opportunities
1. Expanding personal gift market	1. Build consumer preference for personalised gifts
2. Multiple repeat purchases of product for other outlets operated by initial purchasers	2. Sell benefits
3. Unrestricted operating hours	3. Target diverse range of users
4. Increasing awareness of specialty products	4. Educating more potential customers about our products
5. Other markets (domestic and international)	5. Ease, quality and consistency of produce ideal for introduction to the home and wedding gift market
6. Scope for innovation in existing market	
7. Creation of new website	6. Commitment to relentless innovation ensures market benchmarks challenged
8. Growth in terms of penetrating the international market	
9. Amway	7. Due to the fact that the World Wide Web is their most important source of information, more people will become aware of Instead of Flowers ... Box It! through the Internet
10. Support from ECI Africa and the Department of Trade and Industry	
	8. Already established clients in the USA and Europe. Build up good relationships with people who will market our products to the American market. Will extend the international market by conducting market research on other international countries
	9. Become part of the extensive catalogue available to Amway clients
	10. Many professional support services available that will be made use of in the future
Threats (outside the business)	**Minimise threats**
1. Competitors and imitation of products	1. Originality protection; currently two main competitors
2. Window of opportunity may be limited	2. Close window before too many competitors enter the market
3. High number of other gift industry competitors	
4. Dealing with multinationals – delay payment process	3. Guaranteed demand through contract with clients and keeping our focus on the company's main products
5. Inflation	4. Letters of credit must be in place to deal effectively with international countries
6. Weak SA rand compared to the US dollar	5. Bargaining power with suppliers
	6. Term contracts with overseas suppliers

Step 8: Apply the marketing mix recipe

We will use the Alex Township of Rhythm Route example below to illustrate the marketing mix or 4 Ps of marketing:

- **Product/Service** – What do you sell or offer to customers?
- **Place** (distribution) – Where are you situated and which areas do you cover?
- **Price** – What does your product or service cost?
- **Promotion** – How will you advertise your product or service and make customers aware of it?

Many authors of textbooks refer to the 7 Ps of marketing and add Physical evidence, People and Processes to the marketing mix.

The Alex Township of Rhythm Route

Product/Service: Alex Township of Rhythm Route offers a number of products to its customers. The route covers some of Alexandra Township's best taverns and shebeens, art and crafts outlets, entertainment experiences and interesting street life. It attempts to capture the vibrancy of the area.

Place (distribution): Alex Township of Rhythm Route is situated only a few minutes from Johannesburg's up-market suburb of Sandton.

Price: It costs R250 for a full-day tour, including breakfast, lunch and dinner at some of the places listed below. There are specials available for groups of more than 20, as well as for students and pensioners.

Promotion: More information about Alex Township of Rhythm Route can be found by visiting the website: www.alextownshiproute.co.za.

Places to visit on the route include:
- the Mandela Yard Precinct, a narrow alleyway leading to the room where former SA President Nelson Mandela once lived in the 1940s;
- the Roman Catholic Church Precinct, a lively district and home to St Hubert's Church;
- Kings Precinct, the centre of an entertainment district;
- Nobuhle hostel, built by the apartheid authorities to house migrant workers;
- Tsutsumani Village, a housing settlement opened during the All Africa Games; and
- River Park, where visitors can view new developments, including the Alexandra Renewal Project.

Step 9: Develop a pre-opening checklist

This sets down planning you must do before the actual start of business activities.

- Are you in the process of registering your business?
- Are you happy with the name of the business or product?
- If you have brands, have you registered them and their logos?
- Have you opened a bank account in the business's name?
- Have you drawn up job descriptions of key personnel?
- Do you have an accountant and attorney in place?
- Have you identified networking organisations that can assist you when you are starting to do business?

Step 10: Identify your financial needs and the chances of making a profit

The million dollar question: translating the plans into cold, hard cash!!
How much money do you need? How much money do you have? How much money can you realistically make?

4.5   THE ELEMENTS OF A BUSINESS PLAN

The following elements are essential to every entrepreneur when he/she is drawing up a business plan. Every possible element is included in this section, but you must identify which elements are applicable to your business and only use those.

4.5.1   Cover and contents page

It is often said that we shouldn't judge a book by its cover, but people do and that is why your front/cover page of your business plan must sell it immediately and include the following information.

- **Name of the business:** Choose a name that will indicate what the business is about; be careful of choosing a name in a different language than English, if your target market is mainly English speaking
- **Type of business:** Start-up, expansion, home-based business; family business or franchise system. Please note it can be a combination of these types
- **Type of business ownership:** Sole proprietor, partnership, close corporation or company
- **The name of the person who prepared the business plan**
- **Name(s) of owner(s) partners, members or shareholders**
- **Work or business address of owner(s)**
- **Work telephone number and facsimile (fax) number**
- **E-mail and website addresses**
- **Logo or emblem**
- **Date when business plan was prepared**

4.5.2 Executive summary (maximum two pages)

Although this section appears first in your business plan, it is important that you actually write it last. You can obviously only write a summary when you have written down all the elements in detail first, i.e. when you have something to summarise. Then you can come back to the executive summary and highlight the most important information, such as:

- historical background explaining how the idea originated;
- a description of your business concept and your business;
- the opportunity and strategy, as defined in chapter 2 of this book;
- the target market and projections;
- the competitive advantage and unique features;
- the economics (break-even point), profitability and harvest potential;
- the entrepreneurial team;
- business goals; and
- a SWOT analysis (please refer to the feasibility study in this chapter, section 4.4).

4.5.3 The industry and the business concept

- The industry
  A thorough explanation must be given of the industry in which you are going to start your business. This will include the current status and trends of the industry in South Africa and internationally, as well as future trends in the industry. Describe your industry. Is it a growth industry? What changes do you foresee in your industry, short term and long term? How will your business be poised to take advantage of them?
- The business and the concept
  The mission and vision of your business must be described in this section, together with the goals within the business.
  - *Mission statement:* Many companies have a brief mission statement, usually in 30 words or less, explaining their reason for existing and their guiding principles. If you want to draft a mission statement, this is a good place to put it in the plan, followed by:
  - *Company goals and objectives:* Goals are destinations – where you want your business to be in the future. Objectives are progress markers along the way to goal achievement. For example, a goal might be to have a healthy, successful company that is a leader in customer service and has a loyal customer following. Objectives might be annual sales targets and some specific measures of customer satisfaction.
- Business philosophy
  What is important to you in business?
- The products/services
  The most important products or services are highlighted and explained in this section. If there are too many products or services, less importnt ones can be mentioned in the addendum at the back of the plan (see below). Describe in depth your products and/or

services (technical specifications, drawings, photos, sales brochures, and other bulky items belong in the addendum). What factors will give you competitive advantages or disadvantages; for example, level of quality or unique or proprietary features? What are the pricing, fee or leasing structures of your products and/or services?

4.5.4 Growth plan

- **Identify new products or services planned for growth**
  Here you have to look in terms of five years ahead in your business and think of potential products or services that you can introduce in that period that will grow your business.
- **Five-year projection for growth**
  In this section, you must also illustrate the amount of money you need to create growth within your business.
- **Financial requirement and personnel for new products**
  More personnel will be needed the more the venture grows and therefore more money will be needed.

4.5.5 Market research and analysis

No matter how good your product and/or service, your venture cannot succeed without effective market research. It is very dangerous to simply assume that you already know about your intended market. You need to do market research to make sure you are on the right track. Use the business planning process as your opportunity to uncover data and question your marketing efforts. Your time will be well spent.

Market research – How?
There are two kinds of market research: primary and secondary.
- **Secondary market research** means using published information to find out about your market such as industry profiles, trade journals, newspapers, magazines, census data and demographic profiles. This type of information is available from public libraries, industry associations, chambers of commerce, vendors who sell to your industry, the Internet and government agencies. Start with your local library. Most librarians are happy to guide you through their business data collection. Also, there are more online sources than you could possibly use.
- **Primary market research** means gathering your own data. For example, you could do your own traffic count at a proposed location, use the yellow pages to identify competitors, and do surveys or focus group interviews to learn about consumer preferences. Professional market research can be very costly, but there are many books available that show small business owners how to do effective research by themselves.

The following factors must be explained in your market research.
- **Customers**
  You have to identify your target market by breaking down the market into homogeneous groups (i.e. groups whose members are similar). For example, determine the demographic

details of the target group such as age, income, social class, gender, education, occupation, location and race.

- **Market size and trends**
  - What is the total size of your market?
  - What percent share of the market will you have? (This is important only if you think you will be a major factor in the market.)
  - What are the trends in your target market – growth trends, trends in consumer preferences, and trends in product development?
  - What is the growth potential and opportunity for a business of your size?
  - What barriers to entry do you face in entering this market with your new business? Some typical ones are:
    - High capital costs
    - High production costs
    - High marketing costs
    - Consumer acceptance/brand recognition
    - Training/skills
    - Unique technology/patents
    - Unions
    - Transport costs
    - Tariff barriers/quotas
    HOW WILL YOU OVERCOME THESE BARRIERS?
  - How could the following factors affect your company?
    - Changes in technology
    - Government regulations
    - Changes in the economy
    - Changes in your industry
    HOW WILL YOU DEAL WITH THESE FACTORS?
- **Competition**
  Describe your competitors' competitive advantage and competitive edges. Use Table 4.1, **Competitive analysis**, given below, to compare your company with your three most important competitors. In the first column are key competitive factors. Since these vary from one industry to another, you may want to customise the list of factors, i.e. only use the ones that apply to your business. In the cell labelled 'My business', state how you honestly think your business will likely appear in customers' minds. Then check whether you think each factor will be a strength or a weakness for your business. Sometimes it is hard to analyse our own weaknesses. Try to be very honest here. Better yet, get some disinterested strangers to assess your business. This can be a real eye-opener. And remember that you cannot be all things to all people. In fact, trying to be causes many business failures, because your efforts become scattered and diluted. You want an honest assessment of your firm's strong and weak points. Now analyse each major competitor. In a few words, state how you think they compare. In the final column, estimate the importance of each competitive factor to your potential customers: 1 = critical; 2 = important; 3 = not so important; 4 = not important at all.

Table 4.1:   Competitive analysis

Factor	My business	Strength	Weakness	Competitor A	Competitor B	Importance to customer
Products						
Price						
Quality						
Selection						
Service						
Reliability						
Stability						
Expertise						
Company reputation						
Location						
Appearance						
Sales method						
Credit policies						
Advertising						
Image						

Having filled out this table, write a short paragraph stating your competitive advantages and disadvantages.

A positioning map can also help to determine how your business compares to those of your competitors. The map compares two different variables such as price (with a range from expensive to inexpensive) and time (quick or slow). Your business is then plotted on the map together with its competitors. Here is an example of a positioning map for the fast food (chicken) industry.

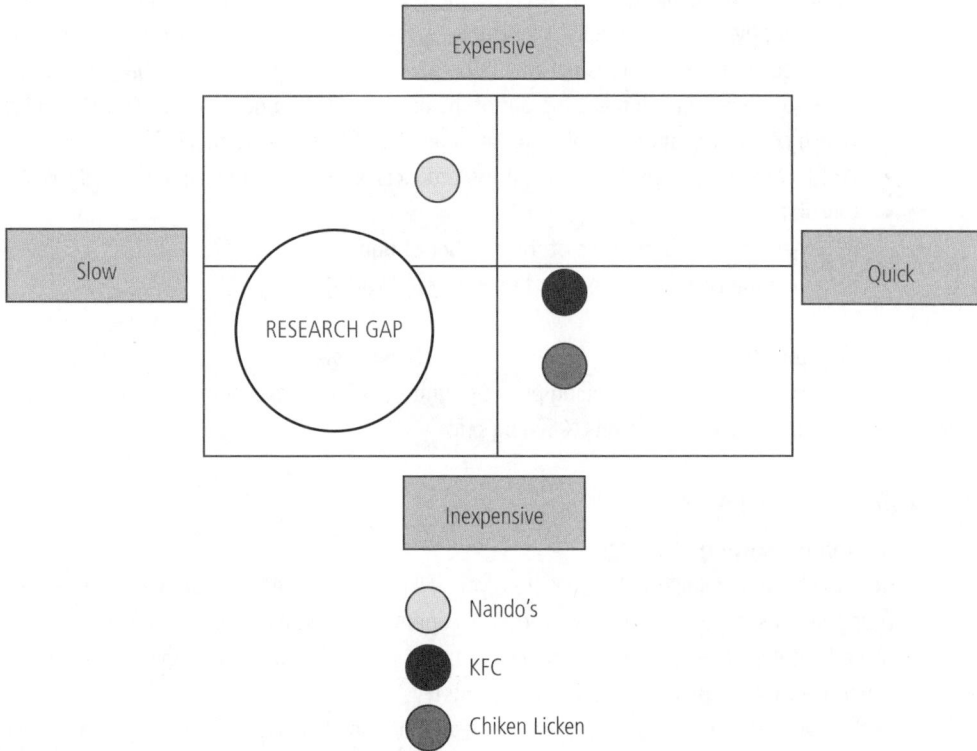

Positioning map: Fast food (chicken)

4.5.6 The economics of your business

Here you must show how you will handle the following financial aspects of your business.

- **Profit potential and durability**
- **Fixed and variable costs**
  - *Fixed cost contributors (these are costs that stay the same, no matter how much you produce or sell)*: Management salaries; wages (and unproductive workers); rent; interest on debt; marketing costs; consulting fees; unnecessary overhead costs, like fuel and entertainment benefits that are unrelated; and uncontrolled pocketing from the cash registers (theft)

- *Variable cost contributors (these are costs that vary according to how much you produce or sell):* cost price of items, inventory levels (how much stock you hold) and distribution costs
- **Months to break-even point**
  - The break-even point is the point when you have covered all your expenses (costs) in your business but do not make a profit. How many products must you sell to break even (the point where profit = R0; loss = R0) and thereafter to make a profit? When will you reach that stage? The moment you sell more products than the break-even point, you will make a profit because there is money left over after all costs in the business have been covered. For example: if you own a hotel and have calculated that you need to have 50 rooms per month occupied to break even and you have 60 rooms occupied, then you will make a profit of the amount you charge for occupying 10 rooms.
  - Which cost **components** make up the total cost of a single product?
  - Which costs are **unavoidable** even if few products or none are sold (i.e. your fixed costs)?
  - Calculation:
    a) when measured in terms of the number of units
    b) when measured in monetary terms (or rand value)

    a) Number of units = $\dfrac{\text{Fixed costs}}{\text{Selling price per unit} - \text{Variable costs per unit}}$

    b) Monetary terms = Units X Selling price

4.5.7 Marketing plan

- **Overall marketing strategy**
  Here you have to detail exactly what steps you will take to ensure that customers know about your product/service and prefer it over the competition. Be as detailed as you can, and give several different tactics (cheapest marketing tactic, proceed to the most expensive, etc.).
- **Pricing – pricing procedures for the industry**
  Explain your method(s) of setting prices. For most small businesses, having the lowest price is not a good policy. It robs you of profits that you will desperately need when you are starting your business; customers may not care as much about price as you think; and large competitors can under-price you anyway. Usually you will do better to have average prices and compete on quality and service. Does your pricing strategy fit in with what was revealed in your competitive analysis? Compare your prices with those of the competition. Are they higher? Lower? The same? Why? How important is price as a competitive factor? Do your intended customers really make their purchase decisions mostly on price? What will be your customer service and credit policies?

  There are three different pricing strategies:
  - *skimming pricing strategy* (when you enter the market with a higher price than your competitors: the aim might be to set the standard for quality; for example, Woolworths follows this pricing strategy);

- *penetrating pricing strategy* (when you enter the market with a lower price than your competitors: the aim is to gain market share, because the competition is very strong; for example, Cell C follows this pricing strategy); and
- *status quo pricing strategy* (when you enter the market with the same prices as your competitors or market-related prices; for example, most franchise systems operate by using this pricing strategy).
- **Sales tactics**
  You must explain the method that you will use to sell your products or services.
- **Service warranty policies**
  This is only applicable to certain businesses that can offer a 'money back guarantee'; for example, if I booked an airline ticket and the plane is full or overbooked, the airline has to put me on another flight and pay for my accommodation if I have to sleep over.
- **Advertising, promotion and distribution: How will you get the word out to customers?**
  In what media, why, and how often will you advertise? Why this mix (i.e. particular combination of advertising methods) and not some other? Have you identified low-cost methods to get the most out of your promotional budget? Will you use methods other than paid advertising, such as trade shows, catalogues, dealer incentives, word of mouth (how will you stimulate it?), networks of friends or professionals? What image do you want to project? How do you want customers to see your business? In addition to advertising, what plans do you have for graphic image support? This includes things like logo design, cards and letterhead, brochures, signage and interior design (if customers come to your place of business). Should you have a system to identify repeat customers, and then systematically contact them?

4.5.8 Design and development plans

- **Development status and tasks**
  If you have products, you have to explain exactly how they look and how they were designed.
- **Difficulties and risks**
  Define any difficulties or risks that you faced while developing the products or services.
- **Product improvement and new products**
  This also forms part of the growth plan for your business, where you have to define which products you will include in your range in the future.
- **Costs, such as:**
  - product development costs;
  - legal costs (registration of trademark or patent);
  - product-testing costs;
  - market research costs;
  - cost of purchasing business premises if you are not renting;
  - cost of machinery and equipment; and
  - unforeseen expenses (such as theft).

- **Proprietary issues**
  This includes any patents and trademarks that you have registered for your business.

4.5.9 Manufacturing and operations plan

- **Operating cycle**
  Here you have to explain how you will operate your business. For example, in the tourism industry you may make use of part-time staff during the low seasons in the year.
- **Geographical location**
  If you already have a location for your business, you should give the physical address and provide reasons why you chose this specific location. If you do not have a business yet and are thinking about a specific location, you should identify the proposed physical address and give reasons why you want that specific site.
- **Contingency plan if your schedule cannot be met**
  A contingency plan is a Plan B or something to fall back on when things go wrong. It is also called a what-if plan.
- **Facilities and improvements**
  Here you list facilities you have that are worth mentioning, as well as improvements that you have made in your business since you started it, or intend to make in the near future.
- **Regulatory and legal issues**
  Any laws, zoning or environmental issues that you have to abide by or register with should be mentioned in this section; for example, if you have a restaurant, you will need a liquor licence.

4.5.10 Management team

Who will manage the business on a day-to-day basis? What experience does that person bring to the business? What special or distinctive competencies does he/she have? Is there a plan for how the business will keep operating if this person leaves or is incapacitated?

If you will have more than about ten employees, draw up an organisational chart showing the management hierarchy and who is responsible for key functions.

Include position descriptions for key employees. If you are seeking loans or investors, then also include resumés of owners and key employees. The following elements must be mentioned.

- **Organisational structure**
  You have to explain on a chart who the key management personnel are and their roles (i.e. what they do in the business).
- **Key management personnel**
  - Include a job description of each person (short CV). Please note that your own CV will be in the addendum at the back of the plan.
  - Include a summary of each person's previous business experience.

- **Management compensation and ownership**
  Give the salaries that will be paid to management, as well as other compensation, such as incentives.
- **Other investors**
  If you have other investors in your business, you have to identify them.
- **Employment, other agreements, stock option and bonus plans**
- **Other shareholders: rights and restrictions**
  For example, you should state if all shareholders do not have the same rights, such as if one is not allowed to sign contracts on his or her own.
- **Supporting professional advisors and services**
  These include people such as an attorney, an accountant, an insurance agent, a banker, consultant(s)and mentors, and key advisors in addition to the above.
- **Board of directors and management advisory board**
  Include this if it is applicable in your business, but this is more for entrepreneurs that own companies.

4.5.11 Overall schedule

In this section, it is important to illustrate what your action plan is going to be for the next six months after you have prepared your business plan. You can make use of a table such as the one below to illustrate your action plan. It is also necessary to illustrate which activity you will be doing at any particular time; for example, market research in months 1–3. Furthermore, it is necessary to indicate whether you will need more employees and money and you must also indicate the deadline for when a particular activity will be completed.

Months	Activity	Employees needed	Capital needed	Deadline
Month 1				
Month 2				
Month 3				
Month 4				
Month 5				
Month 6				

4.5.12 Critical risks, problems and assumptions

- **Identify and discuss any major problems and other risks**
  You must discuss possible pitfalls and how you intend to overcome these; for example, a possible pitfall could be that you grow too fast and run out of cash.

4.5.13 The Financial Plan (ask your accountant for help)

Under this section it is important to include the following statements and financial aspects:

- actual income statements;
- pro forma income statements;
- pro forma balance sheets;
- pro forma cash flow analysis;
- break-even chart;
- cost control; and
- highlights (and avoid 'hidden skeletons').

4.5.14 Proposed company offering

In this section, you have the opportunity to ask for financial assistance, and should give the following information.

- **Required financing:** How much money do you want to borrow from the financial institution?
- **Offering, capitalisation:** What can you offer in return; for example, your securities and assets?
- **Use of funds, investor's returns:** What are you going to do with the money; for example, if you say that you want to borrow R500 000, what will you use if for?

4.5.15 Addendum

This section contains important information that is too long or detailed for the body of the business plan, but which is nonetheless necessary; for example, the entrepreneur's (i.e. your own) CV, press clippings, a list of references, suppliers of critical components, technical analysis, quotations, patents and trademarks, and details of market research. It can also include details and studies used in your business plan; for example:

- brochures and advertising materials;
- industry studies;
- blueprints and plans;
- maps and photos of your business's location;
- magazine or other articles;
- detailed lists of equipment owned or to be purchased;
- copies of leases and contracts;

- letters of support from future customers;
- any other materials needed to support what you have said in your plan; and
- a list of assets available as collateral for a loan.

4.6 THE PRESENTATION OF A BUSINESS PLAN

The way in which you present your business plan is just as important as its content. For example, you cannot show up at a financial institution without your business plan or an appointment with the person you need to see at that institution.

It is important that you remember the following points when you are drawing up your business plan. The plan should be:

- neatly prepared;
- professional in appearance – make it look good;
- concise (don't lose the content in too much frill);
- comprehensive (don't leave out any relevant information);
- logical in its flow of elements, as seen above;
- realistic (be honest);
- easy to read; and
- practical and easy to implement.

4.7 WHY DO BUSINESS PLANS FAIL?

You have now prepared the perfect business plan, or so you think. The reasons why a business plan may not be successful can be one or more of the following.

- You are ill-prepared and show up with a scruffy, three-page document that is supposed to be a business plan.
- You did not prepare the business plan yourself or you were not involved – it was prepared by a business plan writer who knows how to lay out business plans but doesn't know your business.
- Your expectations were unrealistic; for example, you ask for R2 million and can only service (afford to repay) R200 000.
- You have made no commitment to the plan – you still have another job on the side.
- Your goals are unreasonable and/or unmeasurable.
- You have insufficient experience and knowledge to make the plan work.
- You haven't established customer needs – that's why you must do a feasibility study before you write your business plan.

4.8 CONCLUSION

The real value of drawing up a business plan is not having the finished product in your hand; rather, the value lies in the process of research and thinking about your business in a systematic way that is needed in order to draw up a good business plan. The act of planning helps you to thoroughly think through all aspects of your planned business, study and do research when you are not sure of the facts, and look at your ideas critically. This takes time now, but avoids costly, perhaps disastrous, mistakes later.

The outline of the business plan given in this chapter is a generic (general) model suitable for all types of businesses. Obviously, you should modify it to suit your particular circumstances. In this chapter, the elements of the business plan were identified; now the only thing left for you to do is to start preparing your own business plan!

4.9   IMPORTANT NUMBERS TO KEEP AND WEBSITES TO EXPLORE

- The Innovation Fund has guidelines and templates on how to write a business plan, with tips under the link 'Application Procedure' on the right-hand side of the homepage.
  Website: www.innovationfund.ac.za
  Postal address:
  P O Box 2600
  Pretoria
  0001
  Tel: 012-481-4191
- The Department of Trade and Industry (DTI) has some useful links to help you write a business plan and tips on how to start your own business. Search under the 'Starting a Business' link on the right-hand side of the homepage.
  Website: www.dti.gov.za
  Customer Contact Centre: 0861-843-384
  Postal address:
  The DTI
  Private Bag X84
  Pretoria
  0001
- The Business Referral and Information Network (BRAIN) is a website aimed at supplying high-quality information services through existing delivery structures to ensure improvement in the business activities of SMMEs.
  Website: www.brain.org.za
  E-mail address: offersn@namac.co.za
  Tel: 0860-103-703
  Physical address:
  BRAIN National SMME
  Information Centre
  7th Floor 1 Dr Lategan Road Groenkloof
  Pretoria
  0181

- A very brief outline of a business plan is provided by Business Partners.
  Website: www.businesspartners.co.za/Business/Bus info/businfo7.htm
- You can find a more comprehensive checklist to guide your thoughts at the following website:
  www.sba.gov/starting/busplan.txt
- The Youth Portal was designed and developed by the Umsobomvu Youth Fund to provide you with information that can empower you to make informed decisions and choices about your life. Go to the 'Business' link, where you will find advice on writing a business plan and spotting business opportunities.
  Website: www.youthportal.org.za/
  Or you can telephone YouthConnect.
  Tel: 08600 youth (96884)
- Bplans has a great selection of sample business plans. Nothing is more helpful in writing your plan than studying the plans of other real businesses.
  Website: www.bplans.com
- Biz Plan It offers a free Virtual Business Plan, free newsletter, and an advice column called Ask Mr BizPlanIt.
  Website: www.bizplanit.com

5 Assembling the Resources

Felicité Fairer-Wessels

Once you have worked through this chapter, you should be able to:

☞ Decide whether your business should be a sole proprietorship, partnership, close corporation or company

☞ Understand the legal requirements and tax implications of each

☞ Assemble the right team of people for your business

☞ Understand the importance of finance

☞ Know where to get money for your business

☞ Decide about the technology infrastructure for your business

☞ Understand the importance of e-business

This chapter deals with how you should go about getting the best resources to start your new business.

5.1 LEGAL FORMS OF BUSINESS

First of all, it is important to decide what legal form your business is going to take. The legal form of business you decide on will affect all sorts of decisions that you make and affects what you can and cannot do, and also what you have to do in terms of legal requirements, etc. So you should choose the form that will best suit your particular business. There are four choices you can decide from: a sole proprietorship, a partnership, a close corporation, or a private company. All these legal forms of business, with their pros and cons within the tourism context and their tax implications, will be discussed below. However, before you make a decision on what type of business to choose, you should get the advice of a competent lawyer or accountant.

- **Sole proprietorship/sole owner**
  This is best suited to a business that is not fixed-asset driven, but rather service-based, and in which the owner is the sole employee. Here the owner is the person who starts the business and has full responsibility for its operations. Income accrues directly to the owner and there are no complicated statutory (legal) returns (i.e. forms you have to fill in and send off to various government agencies) other than meeting basic legal and tax requirements.

  The disadvantage is that the business is not a separate legal entity from the owner, so the owner is liable for, and can be sued for, the business's debts. If the owner of the business dies, the business ceases to exist.

- **Partnership**
  Based on the same principles as a sole proprietorship, this structure allows you to have up to 20 partners who share responsibility, skills and liability. A partnership requires a contract to formalise each person's contribution to the business, their responsibilities and profit share, procedures to be followed if the partnership changes or is dissolved, the means of resolving disputes, and disability/death insurance.

  In a partnership, there may be some general partnership owners and some limited partnership owners. The first is when two or more individuals have pooled resources to own a business and have unlimited liability; the second is when particular partners have a limited share in the business and therefore limited liability.

- **Close Corporation (CC)**
  This is a popular and widely used structure that gives a business a separate legal identity without the formalities of the Companies Act that governs (Pty) Ltd companies (see below). This structure is ideal for a business that buys stock on credit, because the owner is not liable for and cannot be sued for the CC's debts, except in a very limited way. A CC can have between one and ten members, each of whom owns an agreed percentage of the business and who are jointly liable for managing it properly. A CC can't be owned by a company or be a subsidiary of another CC or company. A CC, rather than its members, can sue and be sued.

  How to register your CC
  - All CCs in South Africa are governed by the Close Corporations Act, which is administered by the Companies and Intellectual Property Registration Office (CIPRO).
  - You can buy CC registration forms from a local stationer, or download them from the CIPRO website www.cipro.co.za.
  - Choose a name for your CC, plus a second and third option in case your first choice is already registered. If you have Internet access, you can check this by using the name search function on www.cipro.co.za/home.
  - Reserve this name by filling in form CK7. Then complete the founding statement form (CK1) in duplicate.

- Obtain written consent from a certified financial accountant to act as your accountant.
- Certain payments must be submitted with the forms (usually under R200) and can be done by direct deposit, electronic transfer, credit or debit card, or cash. See the CIPRO website or call the CIPRO call centre on 0861-843-384 for details. Send the forms, letter and proof of payment to the Close Corporations Registrations Office, P O Box 429, Pretoria 0001 or Block F, The DTI Campus, 77 Meintjies Street, Sunnyside, Pretoria. If the corporation name is approved and all the formal requirements are met, the Registrar will allocate your CC a number. This must appear on all your business documents in addition to the letter CC after the name(Small Capital, May 2005:6).

Liability of owners

Liability is one of the critical reasons for establishing a CC rather than any other form of business.

The proprietor and other partners are liable for all aspects of the business. As the CC is an entity or 'legal person', which is taxable and absorbs liability, the owners are liable only for the amount of their investment.

In the case of a **partnership**, no distinction is made between the business entity and the owner(s). To satisfy any outstanding debts of the business, creditors may seize any assets the owners have outside of the business.(Hisrich, Peters & Shepard, 2005:250–3)

Company

This is also a separate legal entity in which directors are protected from individual liability for the company's debts. A company can make shares available to staff as a private company (which, as you will have seen, puts 'Pty' after its name) or to the public as a limited company (Ltd), and these are easily transferred from one owner to another.

A (Pty) Ltd company has to be audited annually. This is the best legal structure for people who eventually want to sell their business to a large competitor, or list on the stock exchange.

To encourage new and support existing small, medium and micro enterprises (SMMEs), the government has created the following **tax stimulus,** where small businesses will be subject to the following tax structure:

R0 – R35 000 of taxable income	0%
R35 001 – R250 000 of taxable income	10% (aim for this category!)
R250 001+ of taxable income	29%

(GMN Enterprise, 2005:8)

Tax implications

A **sole proprietor** is taxed as an individual, so the more your business earns, the more tax you pay.

In a **partnership**, all partners are taxed as individuals on their share of the profit. The more they earn, the more they pay.

A **close corporation** offers tax benefits in that you can keep retained earnings in the business and delay the payment of tax. However, CCs pay a fixed rate of tax on every rand of profit earned. CCs are treated as companies for taxation purposes (GMN Enterprise, 2005:26).

A **(Pty) Ltd** company pays a constant rate of tax of 29% with financial years ending after 1 April 2005, regardless of income level, and are subject to an annual audit (GMN Enterprise, 2005:26).

Self-study exercises
- Define the various forms of business for yourself.
- Read the following case studies beginning on page 120: 1time Airline, Rovos Rail and Sakhumzi Restaurant; and explain what forms of business would suit them best, irrespective of the form they currently have.

5.2   LEGAL REQUIREMENTS

Every new business has to register with the South African Revenue Services (SARS) for provisional tax, value added tax (VAT), employee tax and the skills development levy.

It is important to remember that SARS regards CCs, companies and trusts as taxpayers in their own right, separate from the individual.

Different tax rules apply depending on the size of your turnover. For example, you are not obliged to register for VAT if your predicted annual earnings are less than R300 000. However, you can and might wish to do so anyway, if the VAT benefit is to your advantage.

If you employ staff, remember to answer the following questions.

- Do you need to pay employee tax – both Standard Income Tax on Employees (SITE) for salaries under R60 000 and Pay-as-You-Earn (PAYE) for those over?
- Are you paying the skills development levy?
- Are you exempted from these two charges? (If the total amount you pay to all staff per year is below the tax threshold of R250 000, you might not have to register for either of the above.)

- Are you paying UIF? (1% of remuneration to be deducted from each employee's salary, and another 1% has to be paid by the employer. This applies even if your staff receive the minimum legal wage.)
- Are you registered with, and paying an annual fee to, the compensation fund (as stipulated in the Compensation for Occupational Injuries and Disease Act)? This applies mainly to manufacturing enterprises.
- Do you have a copy of the Basic Conditions of Employment Act on your premises? (This can be obtained from the Department of Labour.)
- What is the minimum wage you can pay your employees? (This is outlined in the Wage Determination Act, and can be obtained from the Chamber of Commerce.)

As a new business owner, you should also ask your local council what Regional Services Council (RSC) and other compulsory levies you have to pay (such as on sales, wages, salaries and owner's drawings); whether any additional trading licences must be obtained or inspections conducted; and if you need special permission to operate your business in the area.

5.2.1   Tax-cutting tips for small businesses

- *Diarise due payment dates:* This helps avoid paying interest and penalties for late payment.
- *Claim maximum retirement annuity (RA) reductions:* The Income Tax Act allows for a deduction each year for an RA; it also allows an additional deduction of R1 800 per year for RA contributions that are in arrears. An insurance broker will be able to advise you on this. Arrange with your RA fund to make an extra contribution for a previous year in which you did not claim your maximum deduction. You can then claim this payment during the current tax year.
- *Run a tax shelter business:* If you run a business as a sole proprietor from home, you can claim a range of legal deductions, e.g. a portion of your mortgage bond interest, telephone bill, vehicle expenses and entertainment costs. However, the business must generate a small income and have prospects for making a profit in the future.
- *Channel income to your children:* A child is taxed in his/her own right, with a threshold of R21 110 per year. If you pay a salary of less that this to your child for work done, you can claim it as a business expense and your child won't be taxed. Remember that salaries must be in relation to the service rendered and the child must be 15 years or older.
- *Restructure you debt:* Create an owner's loan by selling assets to your business on credit. Use the money the business pays you to settle personal debt, while the business claims the interest it pays on the loan it took to buy the asset. This can be tricky, so get advice from a good tax consultant first.
- *Separate CCs:* When you sell an asset (e.g. a vehicle), you are taxed on the profit you make that is above the tax write-off value. If this asset is in the name of a separate CC, you can sell the whole CC. According to the normal tax rules, the profit made is a capital gain and capital gains tax (CGT) must be paid. CGT applies only to a portion of that profit, rather than the full amount. You should get the advice of a competent lawyer or accountant before doing this, however (Small Capital, May 2005:33).

5.3 HUMAN RESOURCES (HR)

People are one of the most important resources in any business. This is especially the case in the tourism industry, which is a service industry, where the quality of people as a resource and the availability of skilled, committed people is an essential success factor for your tourism business.

Human resources can, on the one hand, be the most crucial problem or, on the other hand, the most important asset for the economic growth and long term sustainability of your business.

5.3.1 The entrepreneurial team

In general, people feel more comfortable around other people who are similar to themselves in various ways. We find that entrepreneurs select co-founders (i.e. people who will help them found or start their businesses) whose background, training and experience match their own. But, it is strategically much better to rather select co-founders with complementary/different knowledge and skills than people with the same skills (complementary knowledge means that one person has one type of knowledge/skill, another person has a different type of knowledge/skill, but put together, their combined knowledge provides all the knowledge/skills a business needs).

In the first instance, as lead entrepreneur, you should conduct a careful self-assessment as part of choosing potential co-founders. You should know what you yourself possess (i.e. your own human capital), and let this determine what you need. You should consider your 'personal resources' such as knowledge, specific skills, motives, commitment and personal attributes – the 'big five dimensions of personality', which include conscientiousness, extraversion-introversion, agreeableness, emotional stability and openness to experience (Mount & Barrick, 1995:153).

The entrepreneurial team consists of a lead/founder entrepreneur and team members who must understand team building; are communicative, passionate and committed; and possess the same team philosophy and attitudes.
The lead entrepreneur must have the capacity to create a dream, crafted into a vision, and must also be able to inspire, persuade and lead people to buy into and deliver the dream – this makes the difference between success and failure, profit and loss.

The team philosophies and attitudes of cohesion and teamwork, integrity, commitment, equality, fairness and sharing should be paramount.

5.3.2 Training and development

In South Africa, the supply of and demand for skills is still very unbalanced in the field of tourism. In some provinces, a large percentage of potentially employable people are not employed because they lack skills and the necessary know-how. It is essential that potential entrepreneurs be equipped with the necessary skills to enable them to create and build new businesses.

The Department of Tourism Management of the University of Pretoria and the CSIR have recently developed the TourGate tourism-knowledge resource system.

This is a user-friendly, easily accessible and integrated information and knowledge system for particularly rural tourism stakeholders to help them improve their decision-making skills. The system is complementary to current initiatives to fulfil a major need for an integrative source of tourism and tourism-related information, not only for existing tourism industry stakeholders wanting to improve their businesses, but also for emerging entrepreneurs and communities wanting to become part of this dynamic and growing industry. It is a web-based tool intended for use by:

- emerging entrepreneurs needing to access relevant, timely and accessible information;
- communities, current tourism businesses and prospective entrepreneurs with the need to access appropriate financial resources for tourism development and marketing;
- rural tourism stakeholders wanting to become part of mainstream tourism by understanding where rural tourism fits into the overall picture of tourism;
- users needing to access relevant information and knowledge on tourism markets, travel patterns and competitive strategies;
- stakeholders needing to determine the true tourism potential of a destination, enabling them to optimise those that are market ready, while creating a tourism investment climate for those with potential;
- stakeholders needing to get clarity on who does what in the industry and to ensure optimal collaboration and co-ordination among stakeholders;
- stakeholders needing to determine the key indicators of success for tourism at the national, provincial, regional, local and business unit levels, so enabling them to use these indicators effectively;
- communities and tourism business units needing assistance in identifying and utilising the processes needed to create access to current and new markets;
- stakeholders needing to monitor trends on a continuous basis in the macro, competitive and market environments;
- users wanting to get access to relevant 'best practice' case studies; and
- users needing to get clarity on the nature and extent of training prospects and to identify career opportunities in the tourism industry (TourGate media release, 7 October 2004).

This system promises to fill a gap in the tourism industry in this regard, especially to build the capacity of people in rural communities and at the grassroots level. Visit it on www.tourgate.co.za.

Common HR mistakes

- No job descriptions drawn up for employees
- Lack of policies and procedures
- Lack of honest communication – you should inform, share ideas, build trust
- Trying to avoid conflict – rather talk it through
- No performance feedback – motivated employees must know the goals of the business and know if they are meeting realistic expectations
- Misunderstanding of probationary periods and lack of contracts – legally all employees must receive written terms and conditions of employment
- Using contract workers to avoid the requirements of legislation
- Lack of a positive management attitude – remember you are all on the same team

Check the labour law ...

Most employers and employees in SA, irrespective of the size of the business, are subject to the provisions of the Basic Conditions of Employment Act (BCEA) and Labour Relations Act.

These laws stipulate the minimum terms on which any employee must be employed, and cover leave, overtime, working hours and payment, among others. They also provide strict guidelines on dismissal, retrenchment and dispute resolution procedures.

For your info ...

Copies of the BCEA (Basic Conditions of Employment Act) and Labour Relations Act can be downloaded from www.labour.gov.za.

This site also has a series of guides written in easy English that explain different aspects of the law. Printed copies can be obtained from regional contact centres.

For the number of the centre nearest to you, call the Labour Department head office on 012-309-4000.

Self-study

- Read the case study on Dyer Island Cruises on page 124. As owner, how would you go about building the capacity of the individuals to add value to the improvement of the lodge.

5.4 FINANCIAL RESOURCES AND GETTING MONEY FOR YOUR BUSINESS

One of the most difficult problems facing an entrepreneur is getting hold of financing for his or her business. Although this is a problem throughout the life of any enterprise, it is particularly difficult at start-up. From the entrepreneur's viewpoint, the longer the business can operate without outside capital, the lower the cost of the capital in terms of interest rates or equity loss in the company. From the viewpoint of the provider of funds, a potential investment opportunity needs to have an appropriate risk/return ratio. A higher return is expected when there is a greater risk involved. The two risks are whether the idea will work and whether the market will accept the product or service the business is selling.

This section describes some common, and some less common sources of capital and the conditions under which money is obtained.

5.4.1 Possible forms of finance before starting your business

As the entrepreneur, you need to decide whether to use debt-based financing or equity, and internal or external funds. What does this mean?

- **Debt-based financing versus equity financing**
  - *Debt-based* (also called asset-based) *financing* usually involves your taking out a loan, on which you will pay interest. The repayment of the amount plus the interest is only indirectly related to the sales and profits of your venture (in other words, you don't pay more or less if your business does well or badly). Debt financing usually requires that one of your assets (e.g. a car, a house) is used as collateral. This means that if you cannot pay back the loan, the item used as collateral will be sold and the money used to repay the loan.
  - *Equity financing* (financing your business yourself or by getting someone to invest in the business), on the other hand, does not require collateral and offers the investor some form of ownership position in the venture (i.e. the investor owns a share of the business). The investor shares in the profits of the venture, as well as any disposition of its assets on a pro rata basis based on the percentage of the business that he/she owns (e.g. if he/she owns 20% of the business, he/she will receive 20% of the profits) (Stutely, 2002:213–14).

Key factors affecting whether it is better to choose one type of financing over another are: how much money is available; the assets of the venture; and the interest rates at the time. Usually an entrepreneur meets financial needs by employing a combination of debt and equity financing.

- **Internal or external funds**
  Financing is available from both internal and external funds. The type of funds most frequently used is internally generated funds, i.e. money that the business actually owns or earns itself. This occurs when the business already exists.

- *Internally generated funds* can come from several sources within the company: profits, sales, reduction in working capital, extended payment terms and accounts receivable.

  In every new venture, the start-up years involve putting all the profits back into the venture, with outside equity investors also not expecting any payback in the early years.

  It is better to rent or lease assets (with an option to buy) than to own them – as long as the level of inflation and rental terms are to your advantage. This will help you conserve cash, which is important during the start-up phase of your company's operations.

  An internal source of funds, on a short-term basis, can be obtained by reducing short-term assets such as inventory, cash, and other working capital items. Care must be taken to ensure good supplier relations and continuous sources of supply in this situation. A final method of internally generating funds is collecting bills (accounts receivable) more quickly.

- *Externally generated funds* are another general source of funds. This funding comes from outside of the company and you need to consider three aspects here: the length of time the funds are available, the costs involved and the amount of company control you will lose as a result.

  The more frequently used sources of funds are: your own money, family and friends, commercial banks, R&D limited partnerships, government loan programmes and grants, venture capital and private placement.

Whenever an entrepreneur deals with items outside the firm, particularly with people and institutions that could become stakeholders, ethical problems can occur.

- **Possible ethical problems you should be wary of:**
  - signs of fraud
  - insufficient working capital or credit
  - extremely high debt
  - dependence on few products, services or customers
  - declining business conditions
  - management dominated by one or a few individuals
  - inexperienced/understaffed financial and accounting functions
  - weak internal control systems
  - rapid turnover of staff in key financial positions/change in auditors
  - unexplained and undocumented transactions
  - apparent tolerance by management of unethical/illegal conduct (Gandoss & Moss Kanter, 2001:415–22).

5.4.2 Getting external funds/financial assistance

Below are listed the different types of funds you can get from a financing institution such as a bank. As we have said already, the greatest challenge for every entrepreneur is getting finance for a small business.

- **A business term loan** is quite an easy way to get hold of funds from about R50 000 for any period up to eight years, and is repayable in equal monthly instalments. This loan can be used to buy assets, increase the cash available to you or buy a small business. The loan period is not fixed and is determined by your monthly payments (i.e. the less you pay each month, the longer you will pay for).
- **An overdraft** on your current account is simple and easy to arrange. As the cash is instantly available when you need it, it aids cash-flow management. Remember that the interest rate on an overdraft is high and using it for a long period can add to your overheads (costs).
- **A business revolving credit plan** is a loan where repayments are made in equal monthly instalments. Once you have paid back a portion of the loan (usually about 25%), you can withdraw the funds up to the original limit. The fixed monthly payments make for easy cash-flow planning. Once again, interest rates may be high.
- **A medium-term loan** has payment options that are structured flexibly in line with your cash flow and is usually paid off over 2–7 years. This loan is suitable for big capital expenses and is usually linked to the prime interest rate. The size of the loan depends on how much collateral you have.
- **A business mortgage** (up to about R5 million) can be used to buy a 'residential' property for use as business premises. The loan is normally for up to 80% of the property's assessed value and is repaid over 15–20 years. You must maintain the potential to convert the property back to residential use when you no longer need it for your business.
- **A commercial property loan** offers long-term finance for the purchase or building of commercial or industrial premises such as shops, offices, warehouses and sectional title units or complexes zoned for business purposes. This loan also covers existing residential properties that are primarily used for business purposes and that have business rights.

5.4.3 Getting finance if you don't have collateral

If you don't have enough security to qualify for a normal bank loan, the following sources of funding exist.

- **Guaranteed loans**
  Khula Enterprise Finance Limited is a government agency that enables local banks and finance institutions to provide collateral-free loans to SMMEs. Khula will guarantee up to 80% of a bank loan on behalf of a small business that does not have assets to put up as collateral. To qualify for a Khula-supported loan you have to meet the normal banking requirements and provide a 10% deposit. For information, contact your nearest bank or contact Khula toll-free on 0800-118-815 or visit www.khula.org.za

- **Donors and funding agencies**
  There are agencies that will provide development funds without requiring collateral or repayment if your small business involves innovative research and development or has the potential to make a significant impact in a particular industry. These agencies will provide funding through a government department or through a partnership with a major SA company that has an interest in the research being funded. Visit the website at www.brain.org.za/financing/donors.html

- **Incentive schemes**
  Financial incentives are offered by some organisations, such as reduced interest rates and payment terms, bridging finance, import finance and development or rehabilitation funds. These schemes are usually available if a business establishes new facilities in economically inactive areas, creates significant job opportunities, beneficiates natural resources or uplifts a community or environment (this would be particularly feasible in the tourism industry). Names, descriptions and contact numbers can be found at www.brain.org.za/FINANCING/incentives.html.

- **Venture capital and equity funding**
  This involves the process of getting hold of funds through another company to start or expand your business (usually from R500 000 to R20 million). The company providing the funds expects higher-than-average returns and normally obtains equity (shares) in your business. The SA Venture Capital and Private Equity Association (SAVCA) publishes a directory of members and their investment preferences. You can contact them on 011-885-2666 or www.savca.co.za.

The basic/big 5 in venture capital
Before asking investors to supply you with extra money, make your proposal as appealing as possible by:
1. building a management team with experience and ability;
2. making your business plan stand out with a great idea – but be concise and honest;
3. approaching the right investor who will understand your idea;
4. knowing your market by compiling stats, potential customers, etc.; and
5. networking x 3 – develop relationships with attorneys, accountants, and people who have investor connections. (*Small Capital*, March 2005:15)

If you are borrowing money from family and friends:
- Remember that you need to discuss a financial agreement with them.
- Keep good relations with everyone concerned, as the possibility of failure is always there.
- Do not ask for more than they can afford.
- Remember to keep them regularly updated on the progress of your business – it is their money!

Always be open to their advice and mentoring, even though it may be irritating at times.

In a new venture, you must evaluate what financial resources you need only after you have assessed the opportunity, formed a team and calculated how much money you need. It is important to remember that cash is the lifeblood of a venture when you are analysing its financial requirements. In other words, if you don't have enough money, your business won't work.

Self-study exercise

Read the case study on Dyer Island Cruises on page 124 and explain what strategies for success may have been used to get this venture off the ground.

5.5 TECHNOLOGY INFRASTRUCTURE: HARDWARE AND SOFTWARE

When starting your own small business, you must know what technology you need, and what you want it to do for you. Ask yourself the following questions.

- What computer systems do I need to operate my business, e.g. basic administration or specialised systems such as graphic design or stock management programs?
- What hardware will I need to run these systems? Different software requires different PC operating speeds, memory and storage capacities.
- How will I communicate with the people involved in my business? How often will I need to phone, e-mail or fax them?
- How will the information in my business be used and shared? Do staff need to regularly access information stored on different computers? Then a LAN network may be necessary.
- Do I need to be mobile? Must I be able to access information while away from my office?
- What kind of free help and technical support will I need, and will the supplier I buy from be able to provide it?

5.5.1 Hardware

Take note of the following and make your own list of the **hardware** items that you need.

- **Central processing unit (CPU):** This controls the speed at which a computer processes information. You will need a PC with at least a 450 megahertz (MHz) processor for tasks such as book-keeping and using the Internet. For graphic design or architectural drawings, your will need at least 800 MHz.
- **Random access memory (RAM):** This is where your computer stores the information it is currently working on. More memory enables you to work faster and have more programs open at the same time. Choose at least 64 megabytes (MB) for basic administrative tasks, and double or more if you are using graphics-based software.
- The **hard drive** is where your PC stores your work and programs. PCs usually come with at least a 40 gigabyte (GB) hard-drive, and this is adequate for a basic office machine. Always

try to buy the biggest hard drive you can afford, as the smaller the hard drive, the sooner you will have to upgrade.

- **Monitors**, or screens: Although larger is more expensive, it makes for easier viewing. Size ranges from 14 to 21 inches (measured diagonally), but most people are comfortable with a 15- or 17-inch screen.
- A **keyboard and mouse** should be comfortable to use. Ergonomic keyboards are shaped to the natural alignment of your fingers and wrists, but can be uncomfortable if you don't know the keyboard.
- A **3,5-inch disk drive and CD-Rom/DVD drive** are now standard for PCs. Check that your PC has extra disc drive slots, in case you want to add drives in the future.
- **Sound and graphic cards** allow for processing involving play-back sound and images on a PC. Cards with more built-in memory offer better performance. Your type of business will determine the level of card you need.
- **Clone PCs** should be avoided. Unlike branded machines (e.g. Mecer, Fujitsu, Siemens Computers), the companies that manufacture and sell clones do not invest in extensive research and development. They source components, often at the lowest cost possible, from several suppliers. While clones are generally cheaper, their long-term reliability is questionable and they can cost you more in the long run with downtime that can seriously affect productivity.

5.5.2 Software

The **software** you choose will depend on your type of business. You must therefore decide which operating system you want to use, as not all software runs on all operating systems. Microsoft Windows offers the best all-round business support, flexibility and security and is suited to most business applications. Operating systems usually have a variety of high-quality software included, such as e-mail and Internet browser software, a selection of fonts, etc. When buying specialised software programs, you need to buy licensed copies.

Although most basic administration programs are available in integrated office software suites that can be bought as a single package, you should compare prices and contents of suites available on the market to buy the one that best meets your needs.

A typical office software suite, such as Microsoft Office, should include everything you need to run the financial and administrative aspects of a small business, for example:

- a word-processing package for producing documents (letters, reports, etc.), e.g. MS Word;
- an office spreadsheet program for basic accounting, statistical planning and management, e.g. Excel;
- an office presentation graphics program, e.g. PowerPoint;
- an easy-to-use design and layout program for basic business publishing and marketing materials, e.g. Publishers; and
- e-mail software with contact management features that will allow you to manage e-mail and general communications, calendars, personal and team information, business contacts,

sales opportunities and personalised e-mail marketing campaigns (e.g. Business Contact Manager in Outlook).

Although setting up accounts is possible in a spreadsheet program such as Excel, you may prefer to buy a dedicated accounting package. For sole proprietors, a personal financial package such as Microsoft Money may be good enough. Should you have more complex financial requirements, it would be wise to buy a package that is compatible with the software used by your accountant.

For software information and training options, visit www.microsoft.com/office; www.microsoft.com/money and www.microsoft.com/southafrica/learning (*Small Capital*, March 2005:18–19).

Why your software must be legal!

- *Pirated software costs you more:* Without a manufacturer's warranty you have no technical support; without a valid licence you have no legal recourse.
- *It is sub-standard:* Pirated software often lacks key elements and upgrade options.
- *You can get infected:* Viruses can enter your system through pirated software and corrupt all your data.
- *It is a crime:* Pirating software is a copyright infringement and a form of theft. If caught, you can be heavily fined for a first offence and imprisoned for a second offence.
- Think of your business's reputation!! (*Small Capital*, March 2005:34)

5.5.3 E-business

In this day and age, it's important to get your business online. Decide what your needs are and choose an Internet service provider that will help you grow your connectivity with your business.

Follow these three easy steps.

1. Get yourself connected

Depending on the needs of your business, there are four connectivity options.

1.1 **Analogue dial-up:** This is ideal for the home user and offers a dial-on-demand connection that operates through a normal telephone landline. You pay for the time spent connected and it is the cheapest and most common way of access to e-mail and the Internet. If you are spending over R800 a month on analogue, it's time to upgrade to ISDN.

1.2 **ISDN line:** This is a dial-up connection that is faster and more reliable than analogue. You also pay for the time spent connected and it is suited for using the line for short periods, or for downloading e-mails. If you are spending over R1 200 a month, it's time to upgrade to ADSL.

1.3 **ADSL:** This is a separate digital line and means that you are permanently connected to the Internet. It offers secure, stable and much faster Internet access at a fixed monthly rate, regardless of how often you use it. It also allows you to use the phone and Internet at the same time.

1.4 **Leased line:** This is a dedicated, permanent connection that offers real-time e-mail and Internet access for a fixed monthly cost. Many people can use it simultaneously and it is ideal for business users who spend more that eight hours a day on the Internet.

For ISDN, ADSL and leased line options, you must apply to Telkom for the line to be installed before your service provider can connect you to the Internet.

2. Get yourself a domain name

By registering your own domain name, your business will have a unique address on the Internet. You can use it for your e-mail addresses (e.g. you@companyname.co.za) and for your company website (e.g. www.companyname.co.za). Your service provider can register your domain name for you and you need to renew the name each year. The MWEB Business website has a search facility where you can check whether the domain name you want is available or not. Also see www.megabusiness.co.za/domains.asp.

3. Get a website

The easiest and most cost-effective way to market your products and services to a global audience is by creating and maintaining a website. Many service providers offer website design and hosting services specifically for small businesses, for a minimal once-off fee and a fixed monthly cost. Your service provider can also give detailed statistics of people who accessed your site each day, week or month. The website can also be upgraded at a later stage to include e-commerce capabilities (Lesonsky, 2004:599–607, 615; Small Capital, March

Self-study exercise

Visit the websites (if they have them) of the following case studies and discuss how good/ bad you think they are in terms of attracting you as a potential tourist:
- 1time Airline
- Rovos Rail
- Dyer Island Cruises
- Sakhumzi Restaurant.

2005:20–1).

5.6 SUMMARY AND REVIEW OF KEY POINTS

This chapter has aimed to give you, in straightforward terms, the different legal forms your business can have; their tax implications; the human resources skills, attitudes and training required by a small business; the resources for obtaining money for your business; and the importance of information technology for your business in terms of connectivity and marketing.

5.7 DISCUSSION QUESTIONS

1. Discuss the legal differences between a sole proprietorship, partnership, CC and company.
2. Discuss the tax implications of each of the above forms of business.
3. Explain why it is important to get the right team of people together for your business.
4. Discuss the various forms of finance you might need before you can start your business.
5. Explain the difference between debt-base financing and equity financing.
6. Explain the difference between internally generated and externally generated funds.
7. Discuss ways to obtain financial assistance from a bank.
8. How would you go about getting finance without having collateral?
9. Discuss the importance of choosing the right technology infrastructure for your business.
10. Debate the value of being 'connected' technologically (phones, faxes, e-mail, the Internet).
11. Using an imaginary business, debate the importance of having your own website.

5.8 IF YOU NEED MORE INFORMATION … THESE ARE HELPFUL WEBSITES/ONLINE RESOURCES

5.8.1 Generally helpful sites and what they provide

www.africa.smetoolkit.org/
Free software, forms and tools for small businesses in Africa.

www.small-business-hub.co.za
A meeting place for entrepreneurs and people in small business.

www.bizassist.co.za
A database of businesses offering services or products to one another.

www.bizland.co.za
Applications, services and information that are indispensable to the small business.

www.brain.org.za
The South African Referral and Information Network, which offers value-added information to SMMEs in South Africa.

www.entrepreneur.co.za
Information to support and help develop entrepreneurs.

www.theinnovationhub.co.za
A hi-tech business hub in Gauteng that provides business support to technology-rich and innovation-based businesses through their start-up, survival and growth stages.

www.jumpstart.co.za
Business advice and venture capital for entrepreneurs in the tourism, technology (financial

sector), telecoms and media industries.

www.myownbusiness.co.za
A site within the Moneyweb network that offers support, news and advice to South African entrepreneurs.

www.realbusiness.co.za
Real Business is a printed supplement in *Business Day* newspaper on the third Monday of every month, and has a huge store of online articles to help manage strategy, leadership, marketing, BEE and starting out.

www.seda.org.za
The Small Enterprise Development Agency, a development and support agency operating within the Department of Trade and Industry.

www.thedti.gov.za
The official website of the Department of Trade and Industry.

www.upstarts.co.za
Founded by Mark Shuttleworth, Upstarts provides facilities and business support services to entrepreneurs.

www.gmn.co.za
Overview of the SA Tax System, incorporating announcements made in the national budget delivered on 23 February 2005.

5.8.2 Equipment rental

www.spartan.co.za
A Microsoft-affiliated provider of rental and finance solutions for certain types of technology hardware and software assets. These include rentals, support and maintenance, upgrade options and insurance. Spartan can be contacted on 011-886-0922.

5.8.3 Software vendors

www.microsoft.com/southafrica/solutionware

5.8.4 Training courses

- **Boston Business College**
  Entrepreneurship diploma (small business management, business communications, basic bookkeeping, accounting and advertising, Excel, Word, Windows XP).
  Contact: Braamfontein branch
  Tel: 011-339-2153; fax: 011-339-2158
- **Damelin Management School**
  Small Business Management Certificate (part-time over four months)
  Contact: 14 colleges nationwide

www.damelin.com

- **MWEB Business tutorials**
  PDF format tutorials on getting a business online, access methods, surfing the web, shopping online, Internet banking, security and business mail. Available on the MWEB Quick Reference Guide CD available on request from MWEB Business: Tel: 0860-100-127 (you pay local phone rates anywhere in the country) or e-mail business@mweb.com
- **University of Pretoria**
  www.up.ac.za
- **Wits Business School**
  www.wbs.mgmt.wits.ac.za
- **Your small business partners**
  www.realbusiness.co.za
  www.fujitsu-siemens.co.za
  www.mwebbusiness.co.za
  www.microsoft.com/southafrica/smallbusiness
  www.standardbank.co.za

6 The Management and Growth of Your New Venture

Felicité Fairer-Wessels

Once you have worked through this chapter, you should be able to:

☞ Identify the management skills that are essential for you as a new entrepreneur to start a business

☞ Implement BEE in your business and be aware of its importance for long-term success

☞ Compile a marketing plan, develop your image and market your new business

☞ Develop your resources, manage risk and expand your business

☞ Control your business's finances, keep records and protect your information

☞ Grow your business in terms of outsourcing, franchising and tendering, and be aware of their pros and cons

☞ Network, provide customer service, manage time, behave ethically and be aware of the importance of quality management

☞ Keep your business afloat, or otherwise know how to end it

6.1 INTRODUCTION

This chapter gives a step-by-step guide on how to manage your new business in order for it to grow. It provides the important skills you need to show leadership, develop a healthy organisational culture, manage conflict and work with the people on your team. The importance of BEE (black economic empowerment) is explained, as well as how you can go about finding a suitable partner and investment. Marketing your business effectively is discussed, as well as how to develop your resources and expand the business. Aspects such as financial control and record-keeping, as well as the legal implications involved, are pointed out. Strategic planning skills are addressed, focusing on outsourcing, franchising and tendering in order for your business to grow. In addition, the importance of networking, customer service, time and quality management, and ethics are discussed. Finally, you are briefed on how to keep your new business afloat, as well as how to end it should it be experiencing severe financial problems.

6.2 ESSENTIAL MANAGEMENT SKILLS FOR ENTREPRENEURS

Typically, a good entrepreneur will have developed a solid base and a wide range of management skills and knowledge over a number of years working in different areas (e.g. marketing, finance and communications). It would be unusual for any single entrepreneur to be outstanding in all these areas. More likely, a single entrepreneur will have strengths in one area, such as strong creative problem-solving and people-management skills, as well as some weaknesses. Although it is risky to generalise, entrepreneurs with a technical background are often weak in marketing and general management, whereas entrepreneurs with no technical background are usually weak in this aspect and good in people-management skills.

It is imperative to have a management team with the necessary ingredients, that is, with skills that complement one another. Together, these skills make up a set of essential entrepreneurial skills or competencies, which is also called a success profile.

The art of entrepreneuring involves recognising the skills and know-how needed to succeed in a venture, by being aware of what each team member does or does not know, and then compensating for any skills that are not available.

6.2.1 Skills in building entrepreneurial culture

Effective managers use a consensus approach to build a motivated and committed team. A consensus is a situation where everyone in the business agrees on what to do and how to do it. Effective managers also balance conflicting demands and priorities and manage conflicts.

Such managers need interpersonal or teamwork skills that involve and influence:

- the ability to create, through management, a climate and spirit that encourages high performance, innovation, initiative and calculated risk-taking;
- the ability to understand relationships between leaders and followers and between tasks; and
- the ability to take the lead in appropriate situations, as well as a willingness to manage actively, supervise and control the activities of others (Timmons & Spinelli, 2004:281–2).

6.2.2 Vision and leadership skills

Many entrepreneurs go beyond focusing on objectives relating to task performance (i.e. carrying out specific tasks). Instead they focus on vision – on what they want to achieve, and what their business can become. The lead entrepreneur would employ, amongst others, communication skills to communicate this vision clearly to employees and others, as this can greatly help the growth of new ventures. If the whole team is working towards a shared vision, that vision can be reached.

6.2.3 Conflict and consensus management skills

In management science terms, conflict is generally defined as a process in which one person perceives that another person has taken or will soon take actions that are incompatible with his/her interests, and this takes two basic forms.

- The first is known as *emotional* or *affective conflict*, where a strong element of anger or dislike is introduced into the situation. Here, the people involved take the conflict *personally*. This form of anger generally produces negative results.
- The second kind of conflict, known as *cognitive conflict*, in contrast, is one in which individuals become aware of contrasting ideas, perspectives or interests, and focus on these issues and not on one another as people. In other words, those involved don't take the conflict personally. Research indicates that cognitive conflict can be constructive, and can result in a solution that is acceptable to both sides.

Conflict is important to entrepreneurs and their efforts to build strong successful businesses. Research shows that when *affective conflict* is high between co-founders of a new venture, the venture will probably not perform well (Ensley, Pearson & Amason, 2002:365–86). Obviously you should try to avoid such situations in your business. However, you need to be able to manage affective conflict effectively when it occurs.

Win-win guidelines to manage affective conflict situations
- **Avoid tactics that will result in a win-lose approach** (one in which each person involved attempts to maximize his/her own outcomes, i.e. to win, which means the other person has to lose). Tactics to be avoided are:
  (a) *beginning with an extreme initial offer:* i.e. one that is very favourable to the side proposing it; this may put the other party at a disadvantage, but will also generate feelings of anger and resentment;
  (b) *the 'big lie' technique:* i.e. trying to convince the other side that you want much more than you actually do, so that they offer more than would otherwise be the case; and
  (c) *convincing the other side that you have an 'out':* if they won't make a deal with you, you can go elsewhere and get better terms.
  These and related strategies tend to jeopardise the situation and are counterproductive in terms of reducing the intensity of affective conflict.
- **Uncover the real issues.**
- **Broaden the scope of the issues being considered:** Often people negotiating are concerned about several issues at the same time. This means trade-offs are possible between those involved; for example, the entrepreneur may be willing to make concessions with an employee regarding working hours rather than salary or fringe benefits, etc. (Baron & Shane, 2005:303).

It is best to avoid affective conflicts within a new venture, as the potential costs are simply too high!

6.2.4 Teamwork and people management skills

As the venture grows, it changes. Managing change is a complex task that is better undertaken with a *participative* style of management. Here the lead entrepreneur involves others in the decision-making process.

In most cultures, employees enjoy the added responsibility of making decisions and taking initiatives that increase job satisfaction.

The list below captures some activities that you as entrepreneur can introduce to create a more participative style of management and successfully grow your business:

- establish a team spirit;
- communicate with employees;
- provide feedback;
- delegate some responsibility to others; and
- provide continuous training for employees.

Self-study

Assess which of your management skills are particularly strong and which are particularly weak. Use the checklists that follow to rate yourself.

The management skills checklist

General management skills	Very strong	Strong	Average	Weak	Very weak
Problem-solving					
Communications					
Planning					
Decision-making					
Project management					
Negotiating					
Managing outside professionals					
Personnel administration					
Management information systems					
Computer skills					

Marketing skills	Very strong	Strong	Average	Weak	Very weak
Market research & evaluation					
Marketing planning					
Product pricing					
Sales management					
Direct selling					
Service management					
Distribution management					
Product management					
New product planning					

Finance skills	Very strong	Strong	Average	Weak	Very weak
Raising capital					
Managing cash flow					
Credit & debt collection management					
Short-term finance					
Public & private offering					
Book-keeping, accounting & control					
Other specific skills					

Operations skills	Very strong	Strong	Average	Weak	Very weak
Manufacturing management					
Inventory control					
Cost analysis & control					
Quality control					
Production scheduling & control					
Purchasing (buying) of stock					
Job evaluation					

Law & tax skills	Very strong	Strong	Average	Weak	Very weak
Companies Act & CC Act					
Contract law					
Patent & proprietary rights					
Tax law					
Real estate law					
Bankruptcy law					
Unique skills					

(adapted from Timmons & Spinelli, 2004:283–96)

6.3 BLACK ECONOMIC EMPOWERMENT (BEE)

BEE or black economic empowerment is an integral part of South Africa's transformation process, which attempts to put right some of the wrongs of the pre-1994 apartheid system. It encourages the redistribution of wealth and opportunities to previously disadvantaged communities and individuals, including blacks, women and people with disabilities. The empowerment process has been identified as crucial to the future viability of the country's economy.

The BEE Commission defines three categories of black empowerment: a 'black' company is at least 50.1% owned and managed by black people; 'black empowered' firms are at least 25.1% owned and managed by black people; and 'black influenced' firms are 5%–25% black owned and managed, irrespective of size of personnel, finances, etc.

Although BEE is more focused on larger and public companies, all businesses, including SMMEs, should try to develop a BEE strategy. Both local and foreign companies are looking for BEE partners in order to establish working relationships or joint ventures, thereby securing state approval for government contracts. A BEE partner may add ten points onto any government contract (i.e. it would give you a greater chance of winning the contract).

Government expects that all South African businesses must be compliant with regulations regarding BEE by 2014. BEE is seen as a challenge by some, but also as an opportunity by others.

As an entrepreneur, you must regard BEE as a vital part of your business's strategy. It must be seen as an important long-term investment in people and also as an essential component for sustainable growth. In other words, when looking for a BEE partner, you must take a long-term view of the value that will be added to your business by this process. This is not something that brings a short-term return on cash, and immediate financial rewards will not be possible. *This is, however, the only way forward for any business that wants to succeed in the South African market.*

6.3.1 Finding a BEE partner

As an entrepreneur looking for a BEE partner, you should look for attributes such as commitment (in terms of funding), access to funding, previous commercial success and sustainability, a strong reputation, good business contacts, a complementary culture, a strong corporate governance record, and, finally, the potential partner must have matching business needs and be able to add value to your business.

You can investigate the following routes when you are looking for a potential BEE partner:

* *established black investment companies*, as they have the necessary capital resources and a high profile;
* *trade unions*, as they have credibility, influence and grassroots representation;
* *community-based organisations*, as they also have grassroots representation, credibility and commitment;
* *empowerment companies already in existence*, as they have commercial expertise, are credible and can add value;
* *key individuals*, as they have the necessary influence and contacts, as well as capital resources; and
* *members of your own staff/employees*, as they are generally stable, can add value to your business as a partner, are credible and have grassroots representation (*Small Capital*, May 2005:19).

6.3.2 The importance of BEE to your business

As an entrepreneur, you need to analyse and 'score' your current and future BEE position. For this, you need to consult the broad-based BEE Act No. 53 of 2003 that provides transformation charters for particular sectors of the economy, including the tourism sector/industry.

Each charter outlines the BEE targets for the relevant industry, as well as a time line for achieving them. For examples of the sectoral transformation charters and scorecards that have been developed, you can visit the website: www.cliffedekker.co.za/literature/bee/bee_08.htm.

You need to reformulate and balance your business strategy in line with the requirements of BEE, taking into account your clients' needs and shareholders' satisfaction. You should use BEE to create long-term equity value by ensuring that BEE initiatives add strategic value to your business (*Small Capital*, May 2005:18).

6.3.3 Investing in a BEE business

When investors are approached to invest in a business that has a new BEE partner/component, they are normally looking for:

- a strong and committed management team;
- potential for growth;
- synergies between the businesses;
- a healthy cash flow; and
- a lower buy-in price, based on the business's need for a cash injection and their ability to bring new business to the table (*Small Capital*, May 2005:19).

6.3.4 Financing a BEE business

The Standard Bank offers two main types of BEE financing:

- *leveraged finance*, which is provided for existing businesses and big business; and
- *contract finance*, which is provided when small and medium-sized BEE businesses (BSMEs) are awarded contracts by corporate or government, but are unable to access finance as a result of a lack of security and/or equity.

Contact Standard Bank's BEE Division on BEE financing on 011-636-9643 for more information or visit www.standardbank.co.za.

6.4   MARKETING YOUR BUSINESS

Preparatory task

Identify a real customer need and explain why an entrepreneur should seek to develop a product/service that meets a real need.

Although it would seem like an obvious thing to do, surprisingly few entrepreneurs develop products and/or services that meet a real need, and therefore most fail to sell anything or make any money. Why is this? Many entrepreneurs get hooked on an idea without properly researching the market to see whether similar products/services already exist, or whether there is a real need for their product/service.

The key question is: **What does it mean for a *real* customer need to exist?** A real need is when customers have a problem that they want solved, but no existing product/services exist that can do this.

You can only start marketing your business effectively when you are able to do the following.

- **Define you business:** From a customer's point of view, be as brief as possible. What do you want to be known for, or what do you want to accomplish?

- **Identify your unique selling point:** Explain how your product/service is different. Why would customers rather come to you than go elsewhere?
- **Create an image:** Decide on a 'logo' to brand your business. Use either a professional designer or design it yourself. Keep it simple, but it must have impact. Your logo must be able to 'tell' people your company name and convey a positive feeling about your business in two blinks of an eye. Remember, you want emotional buy-in from your customers – your product must appeal to their feelings and emotions.
- **Identify your customers**
  - Who are your ideal customers: in terms of age, income, education level, place of residence?
  - What are their needs and what makes them tick? What is on their wish list (Stutely, 2002:86)?
- **Identify your competitive advantage:** What is your company good at doing; what does it like doing (Stutely, 2002:93)?
- **Build your reputation:** Build credibility, maintain high standards of quality and reliability, and provide professional after-sales service (Lesonsky 2004:489).

The secret of business is knowing something that nobody else knows.

Aristotle Onassis

6.4.1 Marketing tips if you have few funds available:

- Market via e-mail.
- Market via the web.
- Network.
- Form alliances.
- Get listed in the *Yellow Pages* or in specific industrial/commercial directories used by buyers in particular fields (Lesonsky 2004:609–19).

Easy steps to create a marketing plan

- **Position your product:** Is it the right product/service for your market? Do your customers think it's a good deal? How easily can your target customers find this product/service?
- **Brainstorm:** Who are you selling to and what do they need? What distinguishes your product/service from the competition? Which marketing tactics will make your products visible?
- **Listen to customers:** What influences their purchasing decisions? Based on this, what are your strengths, weaknesses (i.e. within the micro-environment of your business), business opportunities and threats (i.e. **P**olitical, **E**conomical, **S**ocial and **T**echnological factors in the macro-environment outside your business that may influence it – the PEST factors)?
- **Draft a plan:** Summarise your market position and goals and objectives, and define what you want to achieve by when. List your target markets and strategies, allocate expenses and resources, identify which marketing channels you will use to attract customers and formulate competitive strategies.

- **Track results:** Create benchmarks to measure whether your marketing efforts are paying off.
- **Review your plan each year.**

(J. Krotz, co-author, *Microsoft Small Business Kit*)

Marketing objectives should be:

- specific;
- measurable;
- achievable;
- realistic; and
- have clear time limits.

6.4.2 Tell-tale signs that you need a new marketing strategy

You should look out for the following signs that could indicate that you should revise your marketing strategy.

- Your customers' awareness levels are dropping (i.e. customers are less aware of your products/services).
- Customers believe that your products are no longer relevant to their needs.
- Customers tell you that the product/service that you are offering is no longer unique.
- Your focus is inward-looking rather than externally focused.
- Your marketing strategy lacks a clear plan of action – what exactly are you going to do to market your product?
- You have nothing new to offer – no new product, service or approach.
- Your marketing strategy lacks depth – don't just sell a meal, sell an experience!
- Your business's personality doesn't come across and there is nothing about your product/ service that makes customers feel they are buying something of value – if people think they are buying value, they think it's worth paying for it.
- You are following others instead of finding your own path – be bold, be unique, be yourself! (*Small Capital*, May 2005:23)

Follow the 80/20 rule when marketing

This rule states that 80% of possible business tends to come from only 20% of the effort put into it. Additionally, the cost of getting new customers is about eight to ten times more than the cost of keeping an existing one.

The crux: Define your 'critical few' customers and target your marketing directly to their needs and your marketing will be far more successful.

(*Small Capital*, March 2005:41)

6.4.3 Corporate image

Remember, IMAGE is everything. People notice it when it's extremely good or extremely bad. Be consistent with your corporate image (i.e. do what you say you are going to do), as it reflects the way your business is perceived by the public, customers, business partners, suppliers and competitors. The following key aspects of corporate image should be reflected in your business approach.

- **Leadership:** Your business should reflect knowledge of the marketplace and earn the respect of other businesses operating in the same area as you.
- **Integrity:** Your products/services should show loyalty, determination, strength and dependability.
- **Innovation:** Your business and marketing should portray your company as creative and able to meet customer needs with the latest and best products and/or services.
- **Value:** Your marketing should suggest that customers get value for money (Lesonsky 2004:274; *Small Capital*, May 2005:42; Stutely, 2002:93).

To develop a corporate image, you do not have to resort to expensive advertising agencies to help you. Software programs such as Microsoft Publisher 2003, PowerPoint and Frontpage have user-friendly, sophisticated capabilities that can help you to easily produce branded marketing material, presentations and even your own website. Visit the Office Online website for training at www.office.microsoft.com.

6.5 RESOURCE DEVELOPMENT, MANAGING RISK AND EXPANSION

All the resources mentioned in the previous chapters, such as human resources, financial resources, technology, information resources, etc. need to be developed continuously and managed.

In addition, you also need to manage **risk** in your business. It is estimated that with no tested plan in place, up to 86% of small/medium-sized businesses fail within three years of a major problem occurring. Have a proper contingency plan in place and allocate the necessary time, staff and funds to prepare for possible emergencies.

6.5.1 Managing risk

One of the biggest risks in small business is that a business's operations usually revolve around one or two key people, without whom the business cannot continue. **Keyman insurance** is simply life insurance on those key people.

Risk is inevitable for a new business, but the trick is to identify potential hazards and known risk factors, and then decide how you'll deal with them if and when they happen. Risk usually comes from the following areas of a business:

- **finance** (such as poor cash flow, bad debt, exchange rate problems, etc.);
- **people** (loss of key staff, inadequate skills or training);
- **technology** (technical failure, loss of data, lack of security);
- **changes in the market** (the introduction of new technologies, changes in customer needs);
- **growth of competitors** (new competitors, competitive products/services);
- **natural disasters**;
- **social threats** (terrorism, loss of life and property, etc.); and
- **loss of utilities and services** (power failure, petrol shortages, no public transport) (Stutely, 2002:223–5).

6.5.2 Expansion

Growth is good for developing a business, but should be a gradual process. Growing should take place at a controlled pace, and you should constantly research whether customers still need/want your product/service. Too rapid growth can be more devastating than not growing at all.

When considering the expansion of your business, you need to ask yourself the following questions:
- Are my competitors expanding?
- Do I have the money?
- How will my customers react to change?
- Have I examined the business environment?
- Can my products be sold at lower prices?

Only if these questions can be answered with a 'yes' can you consider expanding your business.

6.6 FINANCIAL CONTROL, RECORD-KEEPING AND INFORMATION SECURITY

The financial plan, which is an inherent part of the business plan, was discussed in chapter 3 and you will need some knowledge of how to provide appropriate controls to ensure that financial projections and goals are met. Some financial skills are thus necessary for you to manage your business during the early years. Cash flows, the income statement and the balance sheet are the key financial areas that you should carefully manage and control.

Take note of the following to help prevent financial 'growing' pains.
- **Managing cash flow:** Your business's interim income statement can be used to effectively establish cost standards and compare the actual with the budgeted amount for a particular time period. Costs are budgeted based on percentage of net sales. These percentages can then be compared with actual percentages and can be assessed over time to ascertain where tighter cost controls may be necessary.

- **Managing inventory:** This is important during the growth of a new business. Too much inventory to meet customer demands can be a drain on cash flow since your business will have to pay manufacturing, transportation and storage costs for that inventory (stock).
- **Managing fixed assets:** These involve long-term commitments and large investments for a new business. Fixed assets such as equipment will require servicing and insurance and will affect utility costs (electricity, etc.). Instead of buying fixed assets, you can lease them, providing the terms of the lease are to your advantage.
- **Managing costs and profits:** Analysis of the income statement will give you the opportunity to manage and control costs before it's too late.
- **Taxes:** The SA Receiver of Revenue requires you to file end-of-year returns of business. Making use of the services of a tax accountant is recommended.

6.6.1 Record-keeping

Good record-keeping helps you to make informed decisions and comply with legal business and tax requirements. It also involves documenting how much money your business receives and how much goes out, and helps to control cash flow.

The type of record-keeping system you use choose would depend on:
- your particular type of business;
- the size of your business;
- the ownership structure; and
- your own record-keeping skills.

Electronic filing should be used if your business handles large volumes of documents, as this will save you space, time and human resources. Many software programs on the market offer electronic filing and archiving. These will help you to compare, update, cross-reference and automate certain tasks.

Back-up (i.e. keeping copies of important business data and information) should be reliable, simple and as automatic as possible. Think of the following when compiling a back-up strategy.

- What data is stored on you system and how would it affect your business if you were without it for a few hours, days or weeks?
- What back-up medium is most convenient for you? Tape drives are the most popular option for large enterprises, because they are inexpensive, hardy and easy to work. CDs are transportable and convenient for smaller amounts of information, while a designated hard-drive can back up large amounts of data or entire systems. On the other hand, fully automated online server space can be rented from an external company. Operating systems such as Windows have built-in back-up programs that work with any of the above data.

Remember that the potential cost of losing data far outweighs any money or time spent backing up your information.

This means keeping records: consider using a software package to improve the flow of this type of information. A database will increase your business's capacity to hold and process customer and other information and will form the basis of the intellectual capital property of your firm.

With a growing business, it may be necessary to enlist the support and services of an accountant or consultant to help you with record-keeping and financial control, and he/she can be used to train your firm's employees.

6.6.2 Legal implications: The ECT Act

The Electronic Communications and Transactions (ECT) Act of 2002 affects the way an organisation stores its information and the way it conducts business on and through the Internet.

The Act covers issues such as the following.

- **Record-keeping**
  Do you record and store all electronic communications and documents as records that could be used as evidence against potential legal claims against your business?
- **Electronic communications**
  E-mail messages, attachments and all their contents are now legally binding, and must be controlled and stored with the same care as any other official business communications.

  Every business owner must know the conditions of the ECT Act. Download a copy from www.gov.za/gazette/acts/2002/a25-02/pdf. Or ask your Internet Service Provider for information and advice to make sure that your website and/or e-mail systems are ECT compliant.
- **e-Filing tax returns to SARS**
  e-Filing is a company that belongs to the South African Revenue Services (SARS) that allows you to submit various tax forms and tax payments online. It operates through a secure line and offers 24-hours-a-day convenience, easy payments, automatic calculations, access to a full history of submissions and payments, a quicker rebate cycle, increased security, no capital outlay and a facility to apply for tax directives. No special software is needed, just a web connection and a standard Windows operating system.

  For more information and to simplify your financial management, contact your bank or SARS on 0860-709-709 or e-mail info@sarsefiling.co.za. Also refer to www.microsoft.com/businesssolutions/solutions.overview.aspx.

What records to keep and for how long

1 year: Cheque stubs, after the annual audit.

3 years: Creditors' ledger, debtors' ledger, vouchers journal, petty cash book, other internal financial documentation, offers of employment, leave forms, increment schedules (personnel), attendance registers, general records and correspondence.

5 years: General ledger reports, employment contracts, general personnel files and personnel loan records.

7 years: Bank statements, vouchers, cashbooks, cheques and cheque requisitions, creditors' invoices/statements, deposit slips, fixed assets register, journal reports, general financial files, petty cash vouchers, sales invoices, confidentiality agreements, leases, guarantees/surety, appointment agreements (e.g. auditors, professional advisors), financial services/banking agreements, cession/assignment agreements, supply agreements, loan agreements, permits and authorisations.

Indefinitely: Annual financial statements, tax returns/assessments, payments made on behalf of personnel, stop orders, Companies Act returns, memoranda and articles of association, special resolutions, minute books, register of company directors/officers, register of directors' interests, register of members, documentation on members' interests, dividend schedules, property ownership titles, prospecting agreements, participation and joint venture agreements, insurance agreements, mining authorisations, trust deeds and personnel benefits.

(*Small Capital*, March 2005:29)

How to control cash flow

- Keep your overheads (expenses) down – it's easier to save costs than grow profit.
- Avoid selling to customers on credit – bad debts can sink a small business quickly.
- Collect debt – follow up as soon as money is due.
- Improve supplier payment terms – negotiate preferential payment terms, etc.
- Keep stock to a minimum – it costs you money to hold stock.

6.6.3 Information security

You need to be aware of the importance of information in your business. You must protect it both internally through a security policy, controls and monitoring systems, and externally through firewalls that prevent external users from accessing any of the computers on your network.

Security issues can become a problem. It is important that you know your employees, as they may develop an anti-company attitude or leave the company and still have a back-door entrance into your critical systems. The better you know them, the easier to take preventative measures. You must train your staff and keep them on your side and 'in the loop' with regard to your security practices. Some 40% of internal security events are errors, accidents or lack of knowledge. Education and awareness are essential.

Tell your staff ...
- Never give out or share user IDs or passwords.
- Be careful not to accidentally give away or lose any business proprietary information.
- Don't connect any computers, modems, etc. to the corporate network without permission.
- Only use licensed and authorised software.
- Protect your workstation, use screen savers and always log off.
- Back up your files regularly, and store back-ups securely.
- Always check mail attachments with anti-virus software.
- Treat e-mail messages carefully and remember that e-mails cannot be 'unsent' once sent.
- Destroy sensitive information that is no longer needed.
- Report security incidents.

(*Small Capital*, March 2005:37)

6.7   STRATEGIC PLANNING SKILLS: GROWING YOUR BUSINESS

I think there is a world market for maybe five computers.

Thomas Watson, chairman of IBM, 1943

When looking for new markets, you must look closely at women and older people. These market segments have the power in terms of number (there are a lot of them), wealth (they have lots of money) and longevity (they live a long time). Ironically, in youth-obsessed America, the mature market controls 70% of all wealth and accounts for 50% of discretionary spending (i.e. money that people have left over to spend after they have paid for all their necessities like food and rent).

Likewise, women are the primary purchasers of nearly everything, says Tom Peters (Re-imagine, 2004) and demand a different approach to marketing, as men and women don't buy for the same reasons: men want to complete the sale, whereas women want to establish a relationship.

To grow your business, you need, amongst others, to:
- employ distributors, sales representatives, dealers, etc.;

- open another location;
- diversify and sell complementary products;
- target a different group of clients;
- merge or acquire another business;
- expand globally;
- reach other markets via e-commerce, i.e. buy and sell online;
- outsource and focus on your core business;
- franchise your idea; and
- tender for relevant projects.

6.7.1 Outsourcing

There will be certain activities in your business that you or your staff are not good at, and they can be outsourced (i.e. you hire someone from outside your business to do them) if:
- it can save you money in the long term;
- it can offer a short-term solution to a problem involving a once-off project;
- it allows a specialised service that is too expensive to employ staff to do within your business;
- it allows you to offer a one-stop-shop service to valued clients; and
- it gives you access to outside expertise and technologies.

Functional areas that can be outsourced are:
- public relations services;
- specialist and expert help (e.g. graphic design, multimedia presentations, bulk mailing, sales and marketing, writing, editing, translation);
- virtual assistants (independent freelance entrepreneurs who provide administrative, creative or technical support);
- e-commerce solutions; and
- e-mail marketing.

Don't outsource if:
- you have enough internal resources;
- you have to abdicate managerial responsibility (i.e. you are no longer in charge of the project);
- you don't have the time to "work" at an outsourced relationship;
- you aren't willing to regard the outsourcing company as a real business partner rather than a simple supplier; and
- there are no clear parameters for costs and over-runs.

6.7.2 Franchising

Franchising can be defined as a method of distributing a product/service and a way of doing business based on a business format/model that is know to work.

The **franchisor** is the company that grants the right to a franchisee to trade under its brand/ trade name. The franchisor has the advantage that its outlets are run by owners driven by the success of their own businesses.

The **franchisee** is the owner who runs the business under the trade name of the franchisor, and has the advantage of running the business through a tried and tested business model/ concept.

Franchising involves money paid upfront and on an ongoing basis to the franchisor and allows use by the franchisee of:
- intellectual property; and
- continuous provision of support and training.

- **How to finance your franchise**
  Very few new entrepreneurs are able to buy a franchise for cash and finance the working capital out of their own pockets. In most cases, you as entrepreneur would approach a bank as a finance partner. The bank, in assessing risk, will determine whether the franchise you want to buy is reputable. In other words, the bank will help you with your pre-buying investigation.

  Standard Bank has a Franchise Desk and can be contacted on e-mail: franchising@ standardbank.co.za.

Interesting facts about franchising …
- The franchising concept was started by the Singer Sewing Company in 1863.
- Coca-Cola followed in 1899.
- Franchising is a significant driver of retail business today and about 12% of retail business in South Africa is done through franchised businesses.
- Some South African examples are: Nando's, Steers, Barcelos – all in the food and hospitality (tourism) industry!
- In South Africa, more than 489 new franchised outlets will be operating by 2010, representing an investment of R489 million and 97,000 new jobs created in the tourism industry.

  (*Business Report*, 18 May 2005:1; *Small Capital*, May 2005:14)

- **Why franchising fails**
  Franchising can fail for the following reasons:
  - the idea is good but the business model/prototype is not easily copied by someone else;
  - the location is bad;

- marketing is poor;
- there is too much competition; and
- expectations may be unrealistic if the franchisee expects to make a profit within a year or two.

6.7.3 Tendering

Why it's important for a small business to tender

- Tenders offer small businesses the opportunity to get access to empowerment benefits, to consolidate, to expand and to grow.
- Tenders are usually put out by government, large public companies, parastatals and municipalities.
- Tenders are a way of inviting businesses to provide goods or services on a contractual basis.

Is your business ready to tender?

- Can you deliver the work according to the specifications, on time and within the budget you have proposed?
- Do you have the experience to deliver goods and services of consistent quality?
- Do you have the necessary resources to complete the work 100% (i.e. cash flow, qualified staff members)?
- Is your business registered?
- Do you have a bank account and record?
- Are you a registered taxpayer with SARS and have you paid up outstanding taxes?

If you cannot answer these questions with a 'yes', your business is not ready to apply for a tender.

If you think your business is ready to tender, you must:
- be honest about your capabilities when filling in the tender form;
- explain the value-for-money or the benefits you can offer;
- be absolutely meticulous and without error when you fill in the tender application;
- be prompt with delivery of your tender document on the 'due' date;
- be able to provide proof of experience;
- be realistic when determining the tender price (i.e. what you are expecting to be paid for the work);
- include your VAT registration number; and
- include project delivery dates and times, as well as samples of your products or brochures, etc.

Note! Remember that when your business wins a tender, you are entering into a legal and binding contract, and this requires you to complete the work as set out in the tender.

Also remember that rushing into a tender can cripple your business and lead to breach of contract.

Bidding for a tender can be exciting, but don't bank on winning each time you bid; rather see each tender as part of a learning curve.

Where tender adverts can be found:
- Major tenders are advertised in the *Government Tender Bulletin* on www.info.gov.sa/ documents/tenders/index.htm.
- Tender Advice Centres (TACs) are NGOs that help smaller businesses access tender information. See www.brain.org.za.

6.7.4 Networking and support – business incubators

Entrepreneurs can use goods and services already available on the market to speed up the pace of their efforts to exploit business opportunities. Sometimes an opportunity is too short-lived for an entrepreneur to put together everything that is needed in time to exploit it. By contracting instead of trying to build everything that you need from scratch, you get the product out quickly and meet the opportunity window.

Therefore entrepreneurs often use already existing goods and services when they are not as good as others at the activities that are necessary to exploit the opportunity. Academics, for example, may invent technologies, but may choose to license their inventions with established firms whose employees have strong marketing skills and business experience (Baron & Shane, 2005:252).

For example, you intend offering a travel service for disabled tourists. Instead of building special facilities, you use accommodation that already meets the needs of disabled people, i.e. wheelchair access, rooms with dedicated appliances, etc. In other words, you source and use the products and services you need for your niche market.

In addition, being quick to market matters a lot when a business faces network externalities (i.e. important contacts that your competitors have and can use to promote their product/ service). These exist when something has increasing value as more people use it. Take *Getaway Magazine* as an example. The more people that read *Getaway*, the more valuable it is. People prefer *Getaway* to *Weg* or other local travel magazines because it already is the largest magazine and reaches the largest reader audience, and is the easiest to use to sell tourism-related goods and services. If a business has network externalities or first mover advantages (i.e. it is the first to put a particular product on the market), entrepreneurs often race to set up these businesses before their competitors.

Personal networks are irreplaceable when you are setting up your own business. Proximity and time are needed to initiate and build personal relationships. Since entrepreneurial activity must cross boundaries, certainly physical ones, and time is a scarce resource for the learning owner-manager, you must develop new ways of networking. Also, the ability to create virtual organisations is becoming increasingly important: the challenge is to build up personal relationships while exploiting modern IT (Sexton & Landström, 2000:376–7).

6.7.5 Customer service/care

Successful entrepreneurs must focus on choosing the right customers to target first, as capital resources are limited in new businesses.

There is no time or money to try and serve many market segments at the same time. The question is: how should you choose where to focus? This involves figuring out which customers need to buy the product/service you offer. Customers need to buy if the product/service gives them something that improves their productivity, reduces their costs, or gives them something that they could not have before (Moore, 1991).

However, to really succeed with your new business, you need to achieve more than a first sale. You need to get a broad range of people to use your new products/services (also refer to chapter 2.8 – How to establish a sustainable competitive edge).

For example, the kulula.com airline addressed the need of many South Africans for cheap flights. Now 1time.com and fly.saa.com have also started penetrating this market.

6.7.6 Time management

This is the process of improving your productivity through more efficient use of time. You gain many benefits from effectively managing your time, such as:
- increased productivity;
- increased job satisfaction;
- improved interpersonal relationships;
- reduced time anxiety and tension; and
- better health.

Basic principles of time management for the entrepreneur
- **The principle of desire:** You should want to change your personal attitudes to the way you do your work and to optimise the way in which you use your time with willpower and motivation.
- **The principle of effectiveness:** You should focus on the most important issues.

- **The principle of analysis:** You need to understand how time is being allocated and where it is used inefficiently.
- **The principle of teamwork:** You need to acknowledge the importance of delegation and to allow others to take responsibility.
- **The principle of prioritised planning:** This requires you to categorise tasks according to how important they are.
- **The principle of re-analysis:** You should periodically review how you manage your time, in order to make sure that you are still using it in the most productive way possible.

(Hisrich, Peters & Shepard, 2005:473–4)

6.7.7 Ethical behaviour

Different ethical behaviour is found in business attitudes and practices in different countries. This area has been explored to some extent within the context of culture and is now beginning to be explored within the more individualised concept of ethics. The concepts of culture and ethics are quite closely related. Whereas ethics is concerned with the 'study of whatever is right and good for humans,' business ethics concerns itself with the investigation of business practices in light of human values.

In short, within the South African situation, with its mix of Western and African values, which include individualism versus communitarian (*'ubuntu'*) values, a Christian heritage versus tribal values, opportunities based on ability versus opportunities created to address previous imbalances, the entrepreneur overall has a social responsibility to employ honest and moral business practices.

6.7.8 Quality management

The International Organisation for Standarisation (ISO) defines quality as 'the totality of features and characteristics of a product or service that bears on its ability to satisfy stated or implied needs.' In a service industry such as tourism, however, the concept of quality still needs to be properly clarified.

Quality is a product-led concept in that it focuses on the features and attributes of the product, and is a measure of to what extent the product or service satisfies the needs and wants of the customer. Unfortunately, quality management is difficult in the tourism industry for various reasons.

- People buy shared use rights to tourism products such as package holidays, and must therefore 'share' their resort with people they do not necessarily like. The behaviour of these other people can negatively affect the tourist's experience of the holiday. In other words, the tour operator has little control over this aspect of the quality of the product.

- People pay very different prices for their holidays; for example, the UK tourism industry offers very low-cost summer sun package holidays. The profit margins are so low on these packages that they don't meet acceptable levels of quality for the average tourist, and many complaints are received about them.
- Customers often have unrealistically high expectations of holidays that a tourism product may not live up to (Swarbrooke, 2003:317–8).

Within the tourism industry, quality management would focus on issues such as:
- the physical environment of a tourist attraction;
- the price the customer pays to use the attraction, i.e. value for money;
- the service offered to visitors by the staff at the attraction;
- the reliability of the product, e.g. whether there are staff shortages, mechanical breakdowns of the roller-coaster at a theme park, menu changes, etc.;
- the safety of the customers visiting the attraction; and
- the number of complaints received from customers (Swarbrooke, 2003:318).

✎ EXERCISES

Self-study exercise
Read the Rovos Rail case study on page 123.

Discuss quality management within a business that focuses on transport, taking both product and service into consideration.

6.8   HOW TO KEEP A NEW VENTURE AFLOAT

- Don't become over-optimistic when your business appears to be successful.
- Always prepare good marketing plans with clear objectives.
- Make good cash projections and avoid over-capitalisation.
- Keep abreast of what is going on in the marketplace (i.e. the rest of the industry).
- Identify stress points and problem areas that can damage your business.

6.9   THE WORST-CASE SCENARIO: ENDING YOUR BUSINESS

Ten reasons why a small business fails:
1. inadequate business planning;
2. insufficient capital;
3. lack of management experience;
4. poor location;
5. poor inventory and cash-flow management;
6. over-investment in fixed assets;
7. poor credit arrangements;
8. personal use of business funds;

9. competition or lack of market knowledge; and
10. low sales/not pricing correctly.

(Small Capital, May 2005:4)*

Once you realise that your business is in severe financial trouble, you have the following options.

- **Bankruptcy:** According to the USA Small Business Administration, about half of all new start-ups fail in their first years. Bankruptcy requires the business to liquidate, either voluntarily or involuntarily. It provides the opportunity to reorganise and make the business more solvent by organising payments to debtors or to end the business.
- **Liquidation:** The most extreme case of bankruptcy requires the entrepreneur to liquidate, either voluntarily (that is when the entrepreneur decides to file for bankruptcy) or involuntarily (when a petition of bankruptcy is filed by creditors without the consent of the entrepreneur), all non-exempt assets of the business.
- **Starting over:** Bankruptcy and liquidation needn't be the end for the entrepreneur. History is full of examples of entrepreneurs failing many times before finally succeeding. Investors tend to look favourably on someone who has failed previously, assuming that he/she will not make the same mistake again.
- **Business turnarounds:** One of the first principles of any successful turnaround has been aggressive hands-on management; the second is to have a plan; and the third principle is the planning process in action involving aggressive corrective action – 'How do we get there?' Time is of the essence either to avoid bankruptcy or to prove to the creditors that you can get your firm back on track.
- **Exit strategy:** Every entrepreneur starting a new venture should have an exit strategy or plan in place at the start-up stage, instead of waiting until it may be too late to put the plan you prefer into effect.

Exit strategies that can be employed are: transfer to family members, transfer to non-family members, employee stock option plan and management buy-out (Hisrich, Peters & Shepard, 2005: chap. 17).

6.10 SUMMARY AND REVIEW OF KEY POINTS

This chapter has aimed to give you the management skills that are essential for you as new entrepreneurs to start a business. It has indicated the importance of implementing BEE in your business and its importance for long-term success. It has given you guidelines on how to: compile a marketing plan, build your corporate image and market your new business; develop your resources, manage risk and expand your business; control the finances and keep the records; grow your business in terms of outsourcing, franchising and tendering; network, provide customer service, manage time, behave ethically and be aware of the importance of quality management; and keep your business afloat, or otherwise end it if all other measures have failed.

6.11 DISCUSSION QUESTIONS

1. Discuss the various management skills that are important in any new business.
2. Explain BEE and its importance for long-term success in a new business.
3. Draw up a marketing plan for your new business.
4. Describe how you would go about developing your resources, managing risk and expanding your business.
5. Explain the importance of financial control, record-keeping and information security.
6. Discuss strategic planning in terms of outsourcing, franchising and tendering in a new business.
7. Explain the need for networking, customer service, ethical behaviour, and time and quality management when running a business.
8. List the steps of keeping a new business afloat, as well as the important measures when this is no longer possible.

Case Studies

CASE STUDY 1: 1TIME AIRLINE

How it all started

Once in a while the time is just right for a good idea to manifest as a reality – the environment is ripe for a new venture to seed, take root and grow. Enterprising people of vision, if they are alert and hungry, see this potential. They act with courage and ingenuity, plant the seed, nurture it and grow it into an enterprise over which other people exclaim: 'Why didn't I think of that first?'

This is what it was like for Gavin Harrison, Glenn Orsmond, Rodney James and Sven Petersen – four entrepreneurial men with a wealth of experience in the aviation industry and a hunger to do things their way: with a no-nonsense integrity.

In 2003, the South African Rand was stronger than it had been for a long time; aircraft acquisition costs were still low in the aftermath of the 9/11 terror attacks; and research proved that low fare, no frills, short haul airlines had been the only successful business model for a number of years, while premium class short haul and domestic airlines were fighting for survival.

South Africa's domestic airline market carries 7 million passengers each year. This market was clearly over-traded with high cost seats and therefore, high airfares. The time for a sustainable, real low fare airline could not have been better. In short, South Africa's first real domestic low fare airline was beckoning to be born.

The perfect foundation was already in place. Through their aviation holding company, Afrisource Holdings, the four entrepreneurs owned Aeronexus – an aviation company that offers aircraft management, crewing and aircraft maintenance services. They realised that this would be an ideal launch pad for setting up an airline.

The team got to work and produced a business plan – that critical document necessary to raise the balance of the funding required to realise their dream. Businessmen were approached and the 50% balance of funding was very quickly taken up. Once again, perfection struck as Mogwele Investments, a black empowerment partner, took 20% and an IT group the remaining 30%. Afrisource Holdings retained 50%. The business model was thus strengthened by diversity and IT skills – aspects without which it is virtually impossible for a modern business to succeed. The availability of key airline executives and managers, with relevant experience, to set up and run the airline was a huge bonus.

On Thursday, 22 January 2004, **1time** opened for ticket sales through the Internet, its call centre, and its ticket sales counters at Johannesburg and Cape Town International Airports. 1time proudly commenced operations on Wednesday, 25 February 2004, with three return flights a day on the Johannesburg/Cape Town route. Since then, the airline has grown from strength to strength, expanding on their initial frequency and incorporating more and more destinations.

The name, **1time** , is a reflection of the South African soul of the company. In South Africa, the phrase **"one time!"** is a colloquialism meaning 'for real!'. The airline's slogan 'Azikho lo nonsense' (no nonsense, or 'no bull') further reflects the airline's determination to sate the public's hunger for a company that is 'for real', with no fine print or terms and conditions on pricing – just the lowest airfares.

The low fare business model

1time was born out of a unique opportunity to launch South Africa's first genuine low fare airline. At that time, it appeared on the surface as if there were already an airline operating in this market but, in order to qualify as an authentic and sustainable low fare airline, a company should be set up from scratch as a low fare model.

An important consideration was the cost of leasing or purchasing aircraft. Low aircraft values due to the 9/11 terror attacks would allow **1time** to either purchase aircraft or to secure long-term aircraft leases at extremely favourable rates. This opportunity was augmented by a strong local currency

Another key factor in the success of the business model was aircraft maintenance. Aeronexus, an aircraft maintenance company with vast experience on the aircraft types identified as ideal for **1time** , is owned by one of the major shareholders of **1time**. Having Aeronexus within the group provides transparency and control, ensuring the highest possible quality, reliability and safety standards.

Standardising on aircraft of a single type ensures simplicity of overall operation, including a single flight crew pool. 1time further provide their employees with pleasant working conditions and incentive-based remuneration, ensuring motivated and productive colleagues.

1time also opted for ticketless air travel, utilising leading edge technology for Internet bookings, call centre reservations, airport check-in, and boarding systems.

1time does not offer the traditional loyalty, or frequent flyer programmes, as these contribute to the high cost of airfares, nor do they give free food and drink – these are sold on board.

1time offers what is believed to be a world first in airline pricing by advertising and guaranteeing its low airfares. Traditionally airlines advertised their lowest available airfares with normal disclaimers such as 'subject to availability' and 'terms and conditions apply'. Consumers generally find that these advertised low fares are available in limited numbers only, have restrictive conditions and contain additional hidden costs. **1time** has broken this convention by advertising its low airfares on an unlimited basis with no additional costs, no hidden conditions and no restrictions.

1time offers consumers a guarantee that its advertised airfares will be offered on every seat, every flight, and every day – irrespective of when the reservation is made.

The growth of 1time shows that the owners did indeed get it right. The 10,000th passenger was carried 20 days into operation and the 50,000th passenger on the 66th day. As **1time** continues to follow the (by now) proven recipe for success, the airline continues to grow with new routes being added on a regular basis and passenger numbers growing steadily.

An empowered company

1time represents the first step in the transformation of privately owned airlines in South Africa. Mogwele Investments owns 20% of 1time. Mogwele Investments is a black empowerment company, represented by Zukile Nomvete and Sipho Twala. Both serve as directors of **1time**, with Nomvete currently assuming the position of chairman of the airline.

Nomvete, in particular, has substantial experience and expertise in the aviation industry. His leadership in the industry is also recognised by his appointment as the Deputy Chairman of the South African Civil Aviation Authority, and his appointment as the South African representative on the ICAO committee on Aviation Environmental Protection.

Chief Executive Officer, Glenn Orsmond, said: '1time is the first privately owned airline to commit itself to the objectives and targets set out in the Aviation Transport Charter. These objectives include a targeted 25% black empowerment shareholding. The airline is furthermore committed to consistently offering the lowest airfares to the general public to make air travel accessible to those previously denied the opportunity to travel by air.'

1time thus becomes the only company in the industry that empowers not only through the diversity of its staff and its shareholders, but also through the community it serves – its passengers.

CASE STUDY 2: ROVOS RAIL

How it all started

Rohan Vos became a rail enthusiast after going on a train trip with his wife. In 1985 he bought his first train coach at an auction with the idea of refurbishing it and hitching it onto South African railways' trains for family holidays.

He then expanded on his original idea and came up with the concept for Rovos Rail. Rohan Vos proceeded to buy more coaches and an engine, which resulted in the company's 'flagship' – The Pride of Africa.

Growth over the last number of years

Rovos Rail has grown considerably since its inception in 1985. The company can now offer trips from Pretoria to Cape Town, Mozambique, Dar es Salaam, Victoria Falls and Namibia. The Pride of Africa can take 72 passengers with its 36 suites.

From the initial staff of one, Rovos Rail now employs 170 people.

Marketing strategies

Rovos Rail employs their own marketing manager, and has various European representatives. Due to the high price of the trips, Rovos Rail has a more exclusive image and does not distribute their products intensively. They use specific distribution channels.

Strategies for success

The Vos family is very involved with the success of the Pride Of Africa. They add a personal touch and unique appeal to the business, with some engines even named after the children of founder Rohan Vos.

The secret to success is found in the entrepreneur Rohan Vos. He integrated his passion for all things mechanical (especially trains) into a business plan that would serve a previously untapped market. He was determined to make a success of his business and he has. He also has a very catching enthusiasm with which he inspires his employees and guests aboard the train.

Barriers encountered

Although Rohan initially struggled with the bureaucracy of the South African Transport Services when he applied for the running of the train and the licence for fare-paying passengers, he refused to be phased by the various times the trains or the tracks broke down, and simply reverted to the ever-ready plan B.

On the 29th of April 1999 Rovos Rail celebrated its 10th anniversary in conjunction with the opening of the newly renovated Capital Hill station in Pretoria, which now constitutes the new headquarters for Rovos Rail.

CASE STUDY 3: DYER ISLAND CRUISES

How it all started

The owner, Mr Wilfred Chivell, has always loved the sea and diving and had a vision to give people a connoisseur's experience of whale watching, by being able to watch from a boat instead of land. He initially started hiring boats to take people on whale sightseeing trips but then borrowed money from private investors to build a special whale watching boat. Due to the company's success, the loan was paid off within a year.

Growth over the last number of years

The company currently employs 12 full time workers, plus additional part time workers during the holiday season.

Marketing strategies

The organisation's web site plays a large role in its marketing strategy, as does Internet advertising. Dyer Island Cruises advertises their community projects and conservation efforts (such as helping rescue penguins after oil spillages) on their web site. This also serves to make visitors aware of these important issues. Clients are able to make online bookings through the web site.

In addition, pamphlets are distributed from various tourism destinations in and around Cape Town.

Strategies for success

According to Mr Chivell, in a tourism organisation such as Dyer Island Cruises, conservation is of utmost importance – according to him 'if you don't look after the natural environment, you might end up without a natural resource to base your business on'.

Mr Chivell has a long relationship with conservation and has worked with various organisations, such as:
- the South African Cultural History Museum
- the Maritime Museum
- the South African Museum in Cape Town
- the Shipwreck Museum in Bredasdorp
- Cape Nature Conservation, particularly with regard to Dyer Island
- Marine and Coastal Management regarding seabirds and marine mammals.

During the slow season, Dyer Island Tours focuses on providing ecomarine trips for marine biologists who are interested in studying the ecology of Dyer Island.

Other relevant information

Mr Chivell believes in Black Economic Empowerment and sees it as one of his success factors. He makes an effort to involve and benefit local communities. He has given two of his friends from the Blompark community a share of 26% in his business, and they are now directors of the company.

Dyer Island Cruises is committed to supporting the local community. Handcrafted cards made by the local rural community are distributed to clients after each boat trip. The community is planning to produce an extensive range of merchandise, which will be marketed through Dyer Island Cruises.

CASE STUDY 4: SAKHUMZI RESTAURANT

How it all started

Sakhumzi opened its doors on 26 November, 2001. The owner had to resign from an IT career in order to raise the capital to start the business.

Initially, the business started slowly. The owner made many mistakes as he didn't have experience of running a restaurant and didn't have the necessary specialist knowledge. He also encountered problems because of a lack of controls. It took 28 months before he began to see an improvement.

Sakhumzi started with 5 employees, but now has a full time staff of 22, with 8 part time workers.

Marketing strategies

Sakhumzi has relied mostly on word-of-mouth recommendations, which means they they must 'do the right thing everyday'. In addition, the owner attends many exhibitions and is now affiliated to associations such as SATSA, Nafcoc and Fedhasa.

Other relevant information

The owner says he has had to learn to be a jack of all trades to get the business running. What has also been a vital ingredient is his own enthusiasm and continued commitment to the project. Any person wanting to start their own business should remember that being one's own boss is not an easy path, and usually takes many sacrifices and lots of hard work.

Glossary

activity: In tourism terms, what people do when visiting outside of their home environment and depending on the purpose for which they travel, either for holiday or business, to visit friends and family or to study.

air transport: The movement of people by air, typically with scheduled or chartered aircraft.

business travel: Travel for purposes that are related to the traveller's work.

demand: Tourists need and motivation for travel; why tourists travel, where they go and what they do.

distributors: In the context of tourism distribution, distributors are those organisations that store information and make it available to intermediaries such as travel agents and tour wholesalers for the buyers of travel services.

cruising: Generally tourist travel on vessels functioning as self-contained resorts targeted at holidaymakers.

cultural attractions: Activities within a country reflecting the way in which people live, work and play, with a focus on artificially constructed environments and the lifestyles of people.

hospitality: The provision of accommodation, food, beverage and gaming services away from home.

industry: In tourism terms, the network of businesses that are engaged in the transport, accommodation, feeding, entertainment and care of tourists.

intermediaries: Any third party or organisation between the producer and consumer that facilitates purchases by transferring the service to the buyer and providing sales revenue to the producer.

leisure travel: Travel for purposes that are related to recreation and holidays.

linkages: Connections between tourists and tourist products and services, both physcially through transport and functionally through the distribution system of travel agents, the Internet and other channels.

natural attractions: Resources, habitat, fauna and flora that are unique and are encountered in a natural state with as little human intervention as possible.

rail transport:	The movement of people by rail.
road transport:	The movement of people by road, typically by vehicles such as cars and coaches.
sea transport:	The movement of people by sea, typically by passenger vessels.
supply:	Products and services offered to tourists to serve their needs when travelling outside their home communities.
tourism:	The activities of persons travelling to and staying in places outside their usual environment for not more than one consecutive year for leisure, business or other purposes.
tourism product:	A combination of all the products and services that make up the tourism experience.
tour wholesalers:	Businesses that put together packages or inclusive tours from the various components of the tourism industry and sell the tours directly to the public or through intermediaries.
travel agency:	Business selling the tourism industry's individual parts or combinations of the parts to consumers.
travel management company:	A travel intermediary that specialises in the business of corporate travel, i.e. the business travel programmes of corporations with a substantial travel expenditure.

CHAPTER 2

attractive:	Used to describe a product or service when it is something that people want or need and will buy.
creative thinking process:	Intellectual process of discovering or inventing new products, services or processes. The creative thinking process can involve inventing new products/services or only changing existing or conventional products/services into improved ones.
creativity:	The ability to recognise ideas that can become entrepreneurial opportunities, which stems from a capacity to see what others do not.
cultural barriers:	Cultural restrictions that inhibit a person from living out his/her creativity.
durable:	Long lasting.
economics:	The money-earning aspect of a new product. The important aspects here are the break-even point (the moment when you will sell enough products or services to cover your costs) and the chance of positive cash flow within two years.
entrepreneurial opportunity:	A situation where an entrepreneur believes that a certain product, service or process has good earning capacity based on the resource inputs that are required to manufacture and market it.
environmental barriers:	Factors in the environment that prevent us from being creative due to the fact that we do not want to be seen as being different or weird.
false assumption:	Goes hand in hand with perceptual barriers, e.g. when a person believes wrongly that he/she is not creative and cannot become creative.

harvest issues:	Issues around when and how the entrepreneur exits the business profitably.
ideas generation:	The process of coming up with new things/concepts that can be developed into opportunities.
innovation:	Innovation supports creativity by always looking for novel, new and improved ways of doing things.
intellectual property:	The ideas basic to a business. This includes ways to protect a good concept, product or service to prevent a competitor from 'stealing' the concept, product or service. These include, patents, trademarks and copyright.
patent:	A registered exclusive right of an inventor to make, use or sell an invention.
perceptual barriers:	An individual's belief that he/she is not creative and that nothing can be done to improve his/her creative skills.
sustainable competitive advantage:	When an entrepreneur has such an edge over his/her competitors that his/her business/product cannot be copied or followed by them.
timely:	Describes the correct time for the entrepreneur to enter the market (normally when competitors in the market leave gaps that the entrepreneur can take advantage of).
trademark:	Word, name, symbol or other device to distinguish goods or services. It is protected for ten years and must be renewed after that period for a further ten years.
window of opportunity:	The time period in which new ventures can be created before too many competitors enter the market.

CHAPTER 3

antecedent influences:	The things from their past that affect entrepreneurs, e.g. their background, family, age, education, work experience, etc.
availability of labour and skills:	Whether skilled workers with the right experience and knowledge needed to operate a business can be easily acquired.
availability of raw material and suppliers:	Whether raw materials needed to run a business can be easily acquired.
climatic conditions:	Conditions such as weather, temperature etc. that affect whether a business can run successfully.
decline/rejuvenation stage:	The product has now reached a low and the need for it is declining. The entrepreneur has two choices: either to let the product die or rejuvenate it by enhancing the marketing as well as innovating the product.
growth stage:	Stage at which the product is known in the market and the business starts to grow.
incubator organisation:	The organisation in which an entrepreneur has previously been working.

introduction stage:	Stage at which the product is introduced into the market for the first time.
location:	The physical place from where a business is run.
maturity stage:	Stage at which the product has reached maturity: it has now stabilised in the market and might need creativity and innovation to keep it popular in the market.
political and social stability:	When a country enjoys political and social stability, it creates a stable environment in which businesses can reach maximum productivity.
product life cycle:	The stages each product or service goes through from introduction to decline; and also the time it takes for a product to move through these stages.
pull factors:	Those factors that encourage entrepreneurship by making it attractive to people.
push factors:	Those factors that encourage entrepreneurship by forcing someone to become an entrepreneur.
seasonality:	The busy and slow times/seasons within a business.
start-up:	The process of establishing a new business in the market.
support and technical infrastructure:	Equipment or machines needed to run a business and support needed if such equipment or machines should break down.
target market:	The market that the entrepreneur will focus his/her marketing strategy on; also known as customers.
transport infrastructure:	Aspects such as roads, public transport, harbours and airports needed to operate a business.
word-of-mouth advertising:	Advertising that takes place through customers communicating information to other people; this can be positive as well as negative.

CHAPTER 4

addendum:	Important information that is too extensive to put in the body of a business plan but which is necessary and relevant.
after-sales relationships:	Keeping in contact with one's customers after they have bought something from your business and providing them with information about your business.
back-up suppliers	Businesses that can supply you if your usual suppliers are not available.
brand identity:	Something that people will recognise and that connects your service or product to a specific logo or slogan.
break-even analysis:	A break-even analysis indicates the point when you have covered all your expenses (costs) in your business but do not make a profit: no money is left over. The moment you sell more products than the break-even point, you will make a profit because there is money left over after all costs in the business are covered.
business plan:	A comprehensive action plan or forecast of how you plan or intend to achieve your business goals. It is a public document and important to the entrepreneur, investors, bankers and employees.

feasibility study:	Assessment of whether the idea for a business will actually work.
competitive analysis:	A breakdown of your competitors' competitive advantage and competitive edge compared to yours.
distribution channels:	The channels that the product/service must go through before it reaches the final users/customers, e.g. retailers, wholesalers etc.
executive summary:	A short summary that explains and highlights the most important information in a business plan.
fixed costs:	Those monthly expenses that stay fixed for a period of at least 12 months, no matter the quantity of goods/services produced.
goals:	Where you want your business to be in the future.
infrastructure:	All the elements needed to start a business, such as location, staff and systems.
marketing mix:	The four key factors that make up the process of marketing, known as the four Ps of marketing: price, place (distribution), product and promotion.
marketing strategies:	A detailed vision of how an entrepreneur will market his/her products or services in order to reach a specific target market.
market share:	The portion left in the market for the entrepreneur to take advantage of once he/she has identified the share that competitors have.
mission statement:	A statement consisting of 30 words or less, explaining the reason for an enterprise being in business and the entrepreneur's guiding principles on how he/she will run and manage the business.
objectives:	Progress markers along the way to goal achievement.
patent:	See glossary for chapter 2.
penetrating price strategy:	When you enter the market with a lower price than your competitors, usually to gain market share because the competition is very strong.
positioning map:	Map/diagram used by an entrepreneur to plot his/her business using different variables in order to compare his/her business against competitors' businesses.
primary market research:	Gathering your own data about the market.
proprietary issues:	Any patents and trademarks registered for a business.
seasonal strategies:	Ways of dealing with the factor of seasonality (see glossary for chapter 3).
secondary market research:	Using published information such as industry profiles, trade journals, newspapers, magazines, census data and demographic profiles to get information about the market. This type of information is available from public libraries, industry associations, chambers of commerce, vendors who sell to your industry and government agencies.
service warranty policy:	Only applicable to businesses that give a money-back guarantee to their customers.
skimming price strategy:	When you enter the market with a higher price than your competitors, usually to set the standard for quality.
supply source:	Source from which you get the supplies needed to run your business.

status quo price strategy:	When you enter the market with the same or market related price than your competitors.
SWOT-analysis:	Determination of the strengths, weaknesses, potential opportunities and potential threats within your business.
target market:	See glossary for Chapter 3.
variable costs:	Those monthly expenses that change or vary depending on the quantity of goods/services produced. The more that are produced, the higher the variable costs.

CHAPTER 5

BCEA:	Basic Conditions of Employment Act.
CC:	See closed corporation.
CGT:	Capital gains tax – a tax on capital gains.
CIPRO:	Companies and Intellectual Property Registration Office.
closed corporation:	A business with a separate legal identity with one to 10 members.
donor:	A person making a gift or transferring property to another person.
lead entrepreneur:	The founding member of an enterprise.
liability:	Amounts owed to the creditors of an organisation that are due to be paid within a certain period.
mortgage:	An interest in property created as a security for a loan or payment of a debt and terminated on payment of the loan or debt.
partnership:	An association of two or more people formed for the purpose of carrying on a business.
PAYE:	Pay As You Earn – a form of income tax.
RSC:	Regional Services Council.
SITE:	Standard Income Tax on Employees – a form of income tax.
SMMEs:	Small, medium and micro enterprises.
TourGate:	A tourism knowledge resource system developed jointly by the University of Pretoria and the Council for Scientific and Industrial Research (CSIR).
venture capital:	Capital invested in a project in which there is a large element of risk; especially money invested in a new venture or an expanding business in exchange for shares in the business.

CHAPTER 6

bankruptcy:	The state of an individual who is unable to pay his debts and against whom a bankruptcy order has been made by a court.
company:	A corporate enterprise that has a legal identity separate from that of its members and operates as one single unit, in the success or failure of which all the members participate.
equity:	A beneficial interest in an asset.
extraversion-introversion:	The degree to which a person is outgoing, assertive and sociable versus being reserved, timid and quiet.

franchise: A licence given to a manufacturer, distributor, trader, etc. to enable him/her to manufacture or sell a named product or service in a particular area for a stated period.

grassroots: Usually community-based rural people who largely focus on their basic needs.

human capital: The 'personal' resources a person brings to a venture, e.g. knowledge of something, specific skills, commitment, etc.

partnership: An association of two or more people formed for the purpose of carrying on a business.

outsource: To employ experts outside of a company to perform certain specialised tasks.

tender: A means of offering services according to certain 'contract' parameters in the hope of securing the contract.

List of Sources

Baron, R.A. & Shane, S.A 2005. *Entrepreneurship: a process perspective*. Mason (Ohio): Thomson South-Western.

Berger, D. 2005. Watch out for new cruising trends. TNW. 1867 (5).

Donald, L., et al. 2000. *The Blackwell handbook of entrepreneurship*. Oxford: Blackwell Publishers.

Birley, S. & Muzyka, D. F. 1997. *Mastering enterprise*. London: Pitman.

Couger, J.D. 1995. *Creative problem solving and opportunity finding*. London: International Thomson.

Ensley, M.D., Pearson, A.W & Amason, A.C. 2002. Understanding the dynamics of new venture performance. *Journal of business venturing*, 17:365-386.

Gandoss, B & Kanter, R. 2001. See no evil, hear no evil, speak no evil – leaders must respond to employee concerns about wrongdoing. *Business and society review* 107 (4): 415-422.

GMN Tax Guide 2005/2006. GMN Enterprise 2005. [www.gmn.co.za]

Hisrich, R.D. & Peters, M.P. 2002. *Entrepreneurship*. 5th Edition. Boston: Irwin/McGraw-Hill.

Hisrich, R.D., Peters, M.P. & Shepard, D.A. 2005. *Entrepreneurship*, 6th Edition. Boston: McGraw-Hill Irwin,

Hjorth, D. 2003. *Rewriting entrepreneurship*. Copenhagen: Liber.

Horner, S. & Swarbrooke, J. 2005. *Leisure Marketing: a global perspective*. Burlington: Elsevier Butterworth-Heinemann.

IATA. 2004. IATA International Cargo and Passenger Forecast 2004 – 2008. [Online] http://www.iata.org/pressroom/industrystats/2004-12-15-03.htm.

Koh, K.Y.1996.The Tourism Entrepreneurial Process: A conceptualisation and implications for research and development. *The Tourism Revue*. 4: pp. 24 – 39.

Lesonsky, R. 2004. *Start your own business*. 3rd Edition: N.P. Entrepreneur Media.

Lubbe, B.A. (ed). 2003. *Tourism Management in Southern Africa*. Cape Town: Pearson.

Lubbe, B.A., Bennett, J.A. & Smuts, C.A. 1998. *Introduction to tourism*. Pretoria: Unisa.

Lumsdaine, E. & Binks, M. 2003. Keep on moving! *Entrepreneurial creativity and effective problem solving.* McGraw Hill Companies [City of publication missing]

Mauzy, J. & Harriman, R. 2003. *Building an inventive organisation*. Harvard Business School Press.

Moore, G. 1991. *Crossing the chasm*. New York: Harper Collins.

Nieman, G.H. & Hough, J., Niewenhuizen, C. 2003. *Entrepreneurship: A South African Perspective*. Pretoria Van Schaik Publishers

O'Connor, P. 1999. Electronic information distribution in tourism and hospitality. Wallingford: CAB International.

Saayman, M. & Saayman, A. 1998. Tourism and the South African economy: Growing opportunities for entrepreneurs. *African Journal for Health, Physical education, Recreation and Dance*. 5:1:1-26.

Sexton, D.L & Landström, H. (ed) 2000. The Blackwell handbook of entrepreneurship. Oxford: Blackwell.

Small capital, a practical guide for small business owners. 2005. Wordsworth, Issue 1 March.

Small capital, a practical guide for small business owners. 2005 Wordsworth, Issue 2 May.

Stutely, R. 2002. *The definitive business plan*. 2nd Edition. London: Prentice Hall.

Swarbrooke, J. 1999. *The development and management of visitor attractions*. 2nd Edition. Oxford: Butterworth-Heineman.

Swarbrooke, J. 2003. *The development and management of visitor attractions*. 2nd Edition. Oxford: Butterworth-Heineman.

Timmons, J .A & Spinelli, S. 2004. *New venture creation: entrepreneurship for the 21st century*. 6th Edition. Boston: McGraw-Hill.

WTTC. 2005. Tourism Satellite Account: Executive Summary. Accessed 24March2005http://www.wttc.org/2005tsa/pdf/Executive%20Summary%202005.pdf

Index